5

Four
Fighters
of
Lincoln
County

Four Fighters of Lincoln County

ROBERT M. UTLEY

CH

The Calvin P. Horn Lectures
in Western History and Culture

University of New Mexico
November 11–14, 1985

UNIVERSITY OF NEW MEXICO PRESS, Albuquerque

Library of Congress Cataloging in Publication Data

Utley, Robert Marshall, 1929–
    Four fighters of Lincoln County.

    "The Calvin P. Horn lectures, University of New
Mexico, November 11–14, 1985."
    Bibliography: p.
    Includes index.
    Contents: Introduction—Alexander McSween—
Billy the Kid—[etc.]
    1. Lincoln County (N.M.)—History. 2. Frontier
and pioneer life—New Mexico—Lincoln County.
3. Lincoln County (N.M.)—Biography. I. Title.
II. Title: Calvin P. Horn lectures, University of
New Mexico.
F802.L7U85 1986   978.9'6404'0922 [B]   86-11218
ISBN 0-8263-0897-X
ISBN 0-8263-0921-6 (deluxe)

Contents

Introduction

One night in June 1982, my historian wife and I watched a television rerun of *Chisum*, featuring John Wayne as the "cattle king of the Pecos," and recounting the adventures, as conceived by Hollywood, of John H. Tunstall, Alex and Susan McSween, and Billy the Kid. Neither of us knew much about the history of the celebrated events that history labels the Lincoln County War, so over the July Fourth weekend we drove down to Lincoln, New Mexico. From our base in the reconstructed Wortley Hotel, we explored the historic old community, which retains in surprising measure the appearance and atmosphere of 1878.

The origins of this volume date from a stroll down Lincoln's only street on that hot July Sunday. Having devoted three decades to Indians and soldiers, I was seeking fresh fields to plow. I found them in Lincoln, a setting for a cast of vivid characters in dramatic conflict and a case study in frontier violence.

The four essays that follow grew out of four lectures delivered at the University of New Mexico, November 11–14, 1985, as Calvin P. Horn Lectures. They do not add up to a history of the Lincoln County War. Rather, they deal with four warriors in that war, each of whom made his own distinct contribution, and each of whom affords a medium for looking at the war from a different perspective. The four are Alexander McSween, Billy the Kid, Lieutenant Colonel Nathan A. M. Dudley, and Governor Lew Wallace. Collectively, they played roles in the war that span its chronology and illustrate its major facets.

Through them, one may gain a reasonably complete understanding of the war.

The path I have followed since Independence Day 1982 in Lincoln has led again, several times, to Lincoln, and also to Tucson, Arizona; Midland, Texas; Denver, Colorado; Washington, D.C.; Albuquerque, New Mexico; and my own home city of Santa Fe. Along the way I have incurred numerous obligations. None has contributed as vitally as Donald R. Lavash, historian at the New Mexico State Records Center and Archives. An authority himself on the Lincoln County War, he pointed the way to key sources, lent me indispensable documents and microfilms from his personal collection (including the Lew Wallace Papers and the Dudley Court Record), and in long sessions over coffee and pastries at the Swiss Bakery shared his insights and helped me sharpen my own thinking. Harwood P. Hinton, editor of *Arizona and the West* and authority on John Chisum, played a similar role. We spent much time together, both at the Haley History Center in Midland, Texas, and at the University of Arizona Library, gnawing at the imponderables of the Lincoln County War.

Others who have contributed in more or less measure, and whose aid I acknowledge with gratitude, are: Beth Schneider, Mrs. Robin McWilliams, and Cindy Burleson at the J. Evetts Haley History Center in Midland, Texas, and of course Evetts Haley himself, both for establishing this fine research institution and for sharing with me his own deep knowledge of the subject; Michael Miller, curator of the Southwest Collection at the New Mexico State Library; David Laird,university librarian, and Louis Hieb, head of Special Collections, University of Arizona Library; Eileen Bolger at the Denver Federal Records Center; Rose Dias at the University of New Mexico Library; Thomas Caperton, director of New Mexico State Monuments; Arthur Olivas and Richard Rucksill at the Museum of New Mexico Library; R. G. Miller, director of Lincoln Properties for the Lincoln County Heritage Trust; John P. Wilson of Las Cruces; and Doyce B. Nunis, Jr., of the University of California at Los Angeles.

At the University of New Mexico, Professor Richard N. Ellis of the Department of History and David V. Holtby of the university press helped lay the groundwork for these lectures and the volume that grew from them. Professors Paul Hutton and Richard Etulain of the Department of History also deserve thanks.

Prominent recognition is due Calvin P. Horn for his sponsorship of the lecture series at the University of New Mexico. Successful businessman and philanthropist, he has also found time and energy to achieve distinction as a historian and publisher of New Mexico history. When he served as president of the Historical Society of New Mexico in 1959, I had the pleasure of working with him as vice president. These Horn lectures afforded opportunity for a pleasant renewal of that association.

Finally, I give thanks to my hardest critic, my wife Melody Webb. Her piercing eye combed every word for clarity and definition and wrought many agonizing revisions.

Santa Fe, New Mexico
November 1985

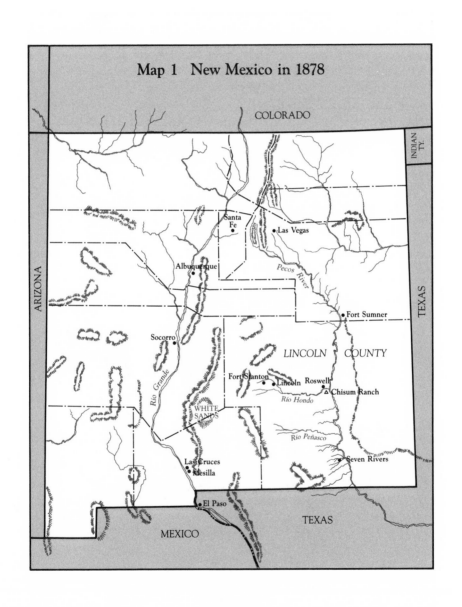

Map 1   New Mexico in 1878

COLORADO

INDIAN TY.

ARIZONA

TEXAS

Santa Fe

Las Vegas

Albuquerque

Pecos River

Socorro

Fort Sumner

LINCOLN   COUNTY

Fort Stanton

Lincoln   Roswell

△ Chisum Ranch

Rio Hondo

Rio Grande

WHITE SANDS

Rio Peñasco

Seven Rivers

Las Cruces
Mesilla

El Paso

TEXAS

MEXICO

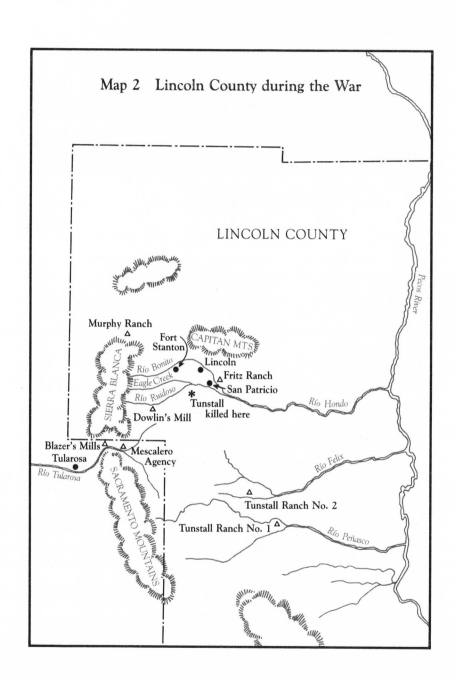

Map 2   Lincoln County during the War

LINCOLN COUNTY

Murphy Ranch

CAPITAN MTS

Fort
Stanton

Lincoln

Río Bonito

Fritz Ranch

Eagle Creek

SIERRA BLANCA

Río Ruidoso

San Patricio

Tunstall
killed here

Río Hondo

Dowlin's Mill

Blazer's Mills

Tularosa

Mescalero
Agency

Río Felix

Río Tularosa

SACRAMENTO MOUNTAINS

Tunstall Ranch No. 2

Tunstall Ranch No. 1

Río Peñasco

Pecos River

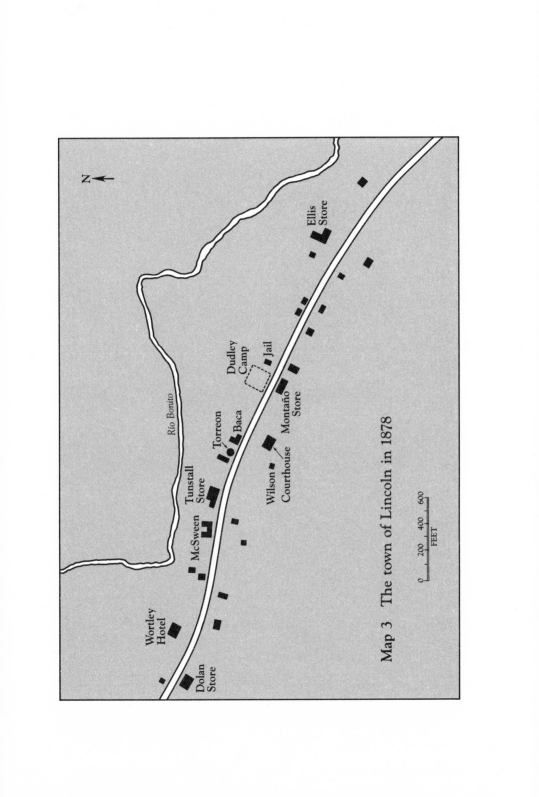

Map 3   The town of Lincoln in 1878

Four
Fighters
of
Lincoln
County

1
Alexander
McSween

Alexander A. McSween, a man of peace, a man of books and words, died by the gun. He died on the doorstep of his own home, backed by men of violence, cut down by men of violence. He rarely carried a gun, yet a small army of gunmen looked to him as their captain in war against another small army of gunmen who had their own captain. McSween's leadership, or lack of it, had brought his army to defeat amid the rude, flat-roofed adobes lining Lincoln's single dusty street. The Lincoln County War did not end in McSween's backyard on the night of July 19, 1878. But the young lawyer's body, torn by five bullets and lighted by the flames of his burning home, marked the end of the first stage of the war.

"Mac" McSween was a central character in the violence that for two years wracked Lincoln County, a huge jurisdiction that sprawled over all of southeastern New Mexico Territory. He may even have been *the* central character. This war was uniquely the making of McSween and the other people who fought it. Economic, political, social, and ethnic forces played their part, but similar forces prevailed elsewhere in the American West during the frontier era without igniting such intense violence. In Lincoln County a handful of vivid characters, driven by impersonal forces common on other frontiers as well, clashed in open and bloody warfare. Alexander McSween contributed decisively to its origin and progress.

Mac and Susan McSween arrived in Lincoln on March 3, 1875, almost three years before the outbreak of hostilities. They were comparatively young—he thirty-one, she two years younger. They came from Kansas but left a dim trail behind them, and they came penniless, "hauled here in a farmer's wagon," as one observer remembered. "He announced his intention of making his El Dorado at Lincoln."[1]

However mysterious their antecedents, the McSweens found a modest El Dorado in Lincoln. He did well enough in his law practice to afford a suitable wardrobe for both of them and to lay plans for a fine new home furnished in the elegant style of the time. In the dusty little village they made a striking couple. Mac dressed in suit and tie, as befitted a frontier barrister. He was asthmatic and had a faintly glassy look in the eyes, but with his mop of curly hair and a mustache that swept like handlebars on each side of a conspicuously long chin, he struck some as handsome. Susan also attracted the attention, not always admiring, of Lincoln's predominantly Hispanic citizens. Piles of carefully curled hair topped a slightly puffy face and a figure a shade ample. Many thought her beautiful, although the impression sprang as much from her dazzling gowns and elaborate makeup as from her physical features. "Mrs. McSween always looked like a big doll," recalled a resident, "she was the best dressed woman in Lincoln."[2]

Prettily situated beside the Río Bonito, Lincoln counted about five hundred residents and served as seat of a county of roughly thirty thousand square miles. Less than two thousand citizens peopled the entire county. They lived in two distinct worlds. In the mountain world, Hispanics and a scattering of Anglos farmed the rich valleys draining the forested high country of the Sierra Blanca and the Capitán Mountains, where Fort Stanton and the Mescalero Apache Indian Agency offered markets for their crops. In the valley world to the east, Texas cattlemen pastured vast herds on the rich grasses of the Pecos Plains and sold beef to New Mexico's forts and Indian agencies. Besides the turbulence normal for a remote frontier with rudimentary government, Lincoln County endured constant tension and sometimes armed conflict born of the historic animosity between the Texans and the New Mexican Hispanics of its two worlds. The McSweens had made their home in a land burdened with a heritage of violence.[3]

At once the McSweens made the acquaintance of Lawrence G. Murphy, head of the powerful institution known simply as "The House." An Irish immigrant and army veteran, "Major" Murphy reigned as economic and political czar of Lincoln County. Fastidiously groomed, attired in black suit and boiled white shirt, with a carefully trimmed red beard and receding hairline framing a face marked by squinting eyes and extraordinarily light complexion, Murphy cut a conspicuous figure on Lincoln's only street. Over the span of a decade, he had come to define and control the economic and political environment of Lincoln County. All citizens lived according to the conditions imposed by this environment.[4]

Murphy's empire rested on government contracts. Santa Fe merchants with Republican connections usually won the contracts for supplying beef, flour, and other necessities to the soldiers at Fort Stanton and the Apaches at the Indian agency. But as the only one in the Fort Stanton area who could consistently guarantee delivery, Democrat Murphy usually ended up as subcontractor. In turn, the contracts enabled him to extend his sway over all of Lincoln County. With lucrative markets of its own at the fort and agency, the company offered a reliable market for farmers and stockmen. Murphy bought their grain and beef to meet his contractual obligations to the government, then sold them household goods, clothing, whiskey, and other merchandise in return. With few competitors to offer a serious challenge, he fixed the prices both of buying and selling. Little cash circulated, and he kept the books that recorded virtually all transactions. Customers complained that he doctored the accounts, but most of them prudently submitted to his reckoning.

Murphy's affable good nature and benign countenance masked unflinching ruthlessness. He held so many people in debt that he could dictate to almost anyone, as he did frequently. He boasted that he controlled the courts, and usually the courts sustained him. "As a matter of business they done as they pleased," said one victim of The House. "They intimidated, oppressed and crushed people who were obliged to deal with them. They were a gigantic monopoly."[5]

Besides Murphy, McSween met his young protégés, James J. Dolan and John H. Riley. They had learned well from their patron. Dolan, a New York Irishman and ex-soldier, worked as clerk and bookkeeper. Like Murphy, he dressed smartly. A mass of dark hair topped a dark-hued, beardless face of distinctly sinister aspect—beady eyes, small nose, and jaws that looked faintly swollen by a perpetual case of mumps. Fiercely loyal, Dolan rose rapidly in his chief's esteem and affection. In 1874, still in his middle twenties, he graduated to a full partnership in The House. Precocious, quick-witted, ambitious for power and wealth, and altogether devoid of scruple, he brought the firm an aggressive drive and competence.[6]

The third leg of The House triangle was another Irishman in his middle twenties, John H. Riley—"a smart devil and a regular confidence man," as one acquaintance viewed him.[7] Riley dealt in beef cattle, in buying them in one place and selling them in another. This specialty made him useful to The House, and in 1876 he became a copartner in The House.[8]

Alexander McSween might well have followed the same path as Dolan and Riley to his El Dorado, and in fact he began his career in Lincoln as Murphy's attorney. But soon he met another man who promised still greater opportunity than Murphy.

An Englishman even younger than Dolan and Riley, John H. Tunstall had family money to invest, and he came to Lincoln late in 1876 in search of an El Dorado infinitely more grand than McSween had dared to dream. In Lincoln he stood forth among the rough-hewn citizenry. Tall and slender, with sandy hair and thin mustache and side-whiskers, he conceded none of his English mannerisms to frontier expectations. He continued to look and act like an educated, cultured aristocrat. Most people welcomed him, for his money if not for his personality, although one cowboy remembered him as "just a damn crazy Englishman."[9]

From McSween, Tunstall promptly learned all about Murphy's operation. Rings, he wrote to his parents, controlled everything in New Mexico. There was an Indian ring, an army ring, a political ring, a legal ring, a Catholic ring, and other rings. In order to succeed, one either had to join a ring or organize one. He chose the latter. "I am at work at present making a ring & have succeeded admirably so far." The purpose of his ring, he proclaimed after meticulous calculations, was "to get the half of every dollar that is made in the county *by anyone.*"[10]

Including himself, Tunstall's ring numbered five men. The charter member was Alexander McSween. Richard M. Brewer, a young rancher from Wisconsin who served as guide and companion in Tunstall's search for a suitable ranch, also signed on early. Lively and engaging, he boasted a more than ordinary intellect combined with both skill and will with a six-shooter. The architects of the ring won a valuable prize in John S. Chisum, the cattle king of the Pecos Valley, who had his own reasons for wanting Murphy neutralized. More than once, Chisum's bids for government beef contracts had been thwarted by Murphy and his Santa Fe allies.[11] The final member of the Tunstall ring was Robert A. Widenmann, a noisy braggart whom Tunstall had taken a liking to in Santa Fe and invited to come down to Lincoln as an all-purpose gadfly.

Altruism motivated Tunstall's ring no more than Murphy's. From the outset, the overriding purpose was to amass a great fortune, in which McSween and the other ring members would share. They sought to liberate the people from the brutal tyranny of The House, but only to substitute their own tyranny, possibly less brutal but no less absolute. The people figured in the scheme only as a source of dollars. As an indignant farmer put it more pithily, "The whole fight was because McSween and Tunstall wanted to run Murphy and Dolan out."[12]

McSween entered into Tunstall's grand design with hope and enthusiasm. It was the means of achieving his El Dorado in Lincoln. He liked the Englishman, and they got along well. Tunstall, in contrast, looked on McSween impersonally, simply as an instrument to aid in accomplishing his ends. "I have worked his affairs & mine in such a shape that they spur him just the way I want him to go," Tunstall wrote in April 1877. And a week later: "I believe I have him in such a shape that he can't slide back a single point; anyhow, he can't make anything by so doing."[13]

The blueprint that McSween helped Tunstall develop and put into effect almost exactly duplicated the one Murphy had followed. Like Murphy, Tunstall acquired a cattle ranch. As a British citizen, he could not homestead on the public domain. But McSween got Dick Brewer and other local residents to file in their names, then consolidated the parcels into a single spread of about twenty-five hundred acres on the Río Félix thirty miles south of Lincoln. Tunstall stocked his range with four hundred head of cattle that McSween picked up for a pittance at a sheriff's auction. Dick Brewer took over as Tunstall's foreman.[14]

The heart of the Tunstall plan was not the ranch, but a mercantile establishment in Lincoln strong enough to compete with Murphy's store. Housed in a new building erected just east of the McSween residence, it opened in August 1877 as J. H. Tunstall & Co., with Rob Widenmann as manager. As part of the store, Tunstall, McSween, and Chisum organized the Lincoln County Bank, with Chisum as president. Never chartered, it consisted mainly of a letterhead unsupported by significant assets, but it provided a mechanism for credit transactions. Besides the store and bank, the new building also housed McSween's law office.

From their new base, Tunstall and McSween reached out to displace The House on every front. They laid plans to seize the government contracts at Fort Stanton and the Mescalero agency. Tunstall spun schemes to land the post tradership at Fort Stanton, and McSween, accusing the Indian agent of fraud, tried to have him replaced with Rob Widenmann. Tunstall devised a system of "grain notes," aimed at cornering the entire yearly crop of corn, wheat, and barley and locking the growers in debt to the Tunstall store.[15]

They may even have toyed with another Murphy technique—filling beef contracts with stolen cattle. At least one rustler swore under oath that Dick Brewer, on behalf of McSween and Tunstall, had offered half the market value and no questions asked for any cattle guaranteed not to have been stolen from John Chisum.[16]

As Tunstall and McSween flung their challenge at The House, they found themselves opposed less by Murphy than by Dolan and Riley. Like many another Lincolnite, Murphy had a habit that proved his undoing. As George Coe put it, "The old man Murphy was dissipated and got so he couldn't do business, just drunk whiskey."[17] In March 1877 he withdrew from the firm. L. G. Murphy & Co. became Jas. J. Dolan & Co., a partnership consisting of Dolan and Riley.[18]

The Tunstall-McSween combination badly alarmed Dolan and Riley, but probably it alone did not cause their downfall. Not until October 1877 did the Tunstall store display more than a meager stock of merchandise. By this time, The House already faced bleak prospects. Business had been declining even under Murphy, and the partners had borrowed heavily to buy him out. In January 1878 they had to mortgage all their property in Lincoln County. While more a future than a present threat, however, the new competitors did provoke Dolan and Riley to fight back with every weapon.[19]

They commanded some deadly weapons. For one, they had their own gang of outlaws, a band of some thirty or forty horse and cattle thieves, known as "The Boys," headed by Lincoln County's most accomplished cutthroat, Jesse Evans. The Boys furnished The House with stolen beef and did other chores to which Dolan and Riley preferred to have no visible link. Rumors flew that McSween and Tunstall had been marked for assassination by The Boys.[20]

Tunstall may have thought he could win over The Boys. Returning from a buying trip to St. Louis in October 1877, he discovered that Evans and his followers had run off some of his and Brewer's choice horses and mules. A posse caught them, however, and lodged them in Lincoln's new jail, a hole in the ground topped by a guardroom of mud-chinked logs. Here Tunstall visited them, exchanged good-natured banter, and even presented them with a bottle of whiskey. On November 17, 1877, they broke out of the jail. Not without reason, Sheriff William Brady accused Tunstall and Brewer of helping them to escape, and in fact The Boys returned the animals they had stolen and promised not to bother Tunstall again.[21]

Another House advantage lay in the courts. If not actually controlled by The House, as Murphy boasted, they at least favored The House. Based in Mesilla, on the Río Grande, Judge Warren Bristol presided over New Mexico's Third Judicial District, serving both as federal and territorial judge and as an associate justice of the territorial supreme court. A meek little man with a bald head, an untidy beard, and a frightened look in his eyes, Bristol tried to be fair and impartial. But sometimes he had a hard time of it, especially when dealing with the likes of Dolan and Riley on their home turf, where he held court twice a year. Not even pretending impartiality, District Attorney William L. Rynerson, a great hairy giant with a fiery temper, shamelessly favored his friend Dolan. Closer to home, Sheriff Brady, a quietly able lawman, had ties to The House that predisposed him toward Dolan and Riley.[22]

McSween's own lapse of judgment gave his enemies their chance to use this advantage. Shortly after arriving in Lincoln, he had taken on the routine legal work of settling the estate of Emil Fritz, Murphy's first partner, who had died in June 1874 during a visit to his home in Germany. Among the debts to the estate that McSween collected were the proceeds of a life insurance policy. For several reasons, including a demand for his own fee, he procrastinated in turning this money over to the administrators of the estate. On December 18, 1877, before the probate court had ruled on the issue, McSween and Susan left Lincoln for a business trip to St. Louis. Declaring that McSween meant to keep the money and never return, Dolan promptly corralled Emilie Scholand, Fritz's sister and administratrix of the Fritz estate, who lived in Las Cruces. On December 21 she filed an affidavit with Judge Bristol in Mesilla charging McSween with embezzlement. Under Dolan's urging, the judge lost no time in issuing an arrest warrant, and the newly strung telegraph wires enabled the fugitive to be intercepted in Las Vegas. Sending Susan on to the East, McSween made ready to go back and defend himself.[23]

If the lawyer thought a simple legal explanation would clear up the matter, he was badly mistaken. With Tunstall and others, including Adolph P. Barrier, a Las Vegas deputy assigned to guard him, McSween appeared before Judge Bristol in Mesilla early in February. Prosecution and defense quickly agreed that, as additional witnesses and documents were needed, the case should be continued to the April term of district court in Lincoln. Judge Bristol set bail at eight thousand dollars, to be approved by District Attorney Rynerson, and instructed McSween's escort to take him back to Lincoln and turn him over to Sheriff Brady, who would hold him until he posted bail.[24]

As the McSween party began the return journey, Dolan remained in Mesilla, busily spinning new webs to ensnare his enemy. When he had finished, Mrs. Scholand and her brother Charles Fritz had sued McSween for ten thousand dollars, and Judge Bristol had issued a writ of attachment against McSween's property. A courier hastened the writ to Dolan, already on his way home, and he traveled day and night to reach Lincoln in advance of McSween.[25]

When McSween and Tunstall reached Lincoln on February 10, they discovered that Sheriff Brady and a posse had entered McSween's home and office, where they had begun to inventory his possessions under the writ of attachment. They had even occupied the Tunstall store and were recording the entire stock of merchandise. Brady based this action on the assumption that Tunstall and McSween were partners and that McSween's share was legally attachable. They were not partners, but Judge Bristol had understood them to say so during the hearing.[26]

Deputy Barrier hesitated to turn McSween over to Brady. The merriment with which the sheriff and Dolan and Riley greeted the prospect of confining McSween worried him. On top of this, McSween's efforts to post bond ran into District Attorney Rynerson's refusal to approve his sureties, a tactic patently contrived to make certain that he spent six weeks in jail awaiting the April term of court. Convinced that to surrender his prisoner would sentence him to execution by The House, Barrier decided to stick with McSween.[27]

With the enemy on the run, Dolan stepped up the offensive. On February 11 Sheriff Brady, still considering Tunstall's property to be partly McSween's, moved against the cattle pastured on Tunstall's ranch. He deputized Jacob B. Mathews, a Dolan lieutenant and silent partner in The House, to organize a posse and attach these cattle. En route, Jesse Evans and two of his thugs joined the posse over Mathews's perfunctory protest. Mathews succeeded, but at the cost of Tunstall's life. Late at night on February 18, Rob Widenmann and other Tunstall minions came to McSween's home with word that he had been killed— shot while supposedly resisting the attachment by Deputy William S. Morton and either Jesse Evans or one of his men.[28]

The shots that felled Tunstall were the opening guns of the Lincoln County War. Even before news came of Tunstall's death, several dozen men had collected at the McSween home.[29] Suddenly, McSween found himself thrust into the command of his own army and expected to avenge what all on his side regarded as the cold-blooded, premeditated murder of Tunstall by men deputized by Brady but paid by Dolan.

McSween's army wanted to fight back. Most strident were those who had been with Tunstall when the posse attacked—Widenmann, Brewer, and three Tunstall hands. One of the hands, a light-hearted, smooth-faced youth, enjoyed a well-deserved reputation for marksmanship and already, though only eighteen, gave evidence of a potential for leadership. His name was William Bonney, but he also went by the name of Antrim, Kid Antrim, or just "Kid."

The Scotch lawyer had no aptitude for their kind of fight. He excelled at manipulating legal, commercial, and financial systems, but he had no experience in fighting a war with guns. Almost alone among Lincolnites, he carried neither rifle nor pistol, and by temperament he shrank from physical combat. Words, not bullets, were his weapons. Demoralized by the maneuvers that had placed him outside the law, he groped for legal rather than violent solutions.

McSween's strategy centered on John B. Wilson, a dull-witted, barely literate old man who presided as justice of the peace of the county's Precinct No. 1. If The House commanded a judicial and law-enforcement system, McSween would oppose it with one of his own. He had affidavits sworn before Wilson and warrants issued charging eighteen members of Mathews's posse, including Dolan, with Tunstall's murder. He also had charges brought against Brady and his men in the Tunstall store for appropriating goods belonging to the Tunstall estate. The murder charges collapsed when Brady simply refused to allow his deputies to be arrested by Wilson's enforcement officer, Constable Atanacio Martínez, and instead arrested him and his deputies.

With the other charges McSween had greater success, due chiefly to Rob Widenmann, Tunstall's erstwhile aide. Widenmann held a commission as deputy United States marshal and carried warrants for the arrest of Jesse Evans and some of his gang for stealing stock on the Indian reservation, a federal offense. On the pretext that Evans and others named in the warrants might be in Lincoln, Widenmann obtained a posse of soldiers at Fort Stanton to help him search for the fugitives.[30] Under cover of the soldiers, Widenmann entered the Tunstall store. He did not find Evans, of course, but Martínez followed with a band of McSween gunmen and arrested all of the Brady deputies on the Wilson warrants. Rather than risk a shootout, Brady never tried to retake the store.[31]

McSween's maneuvers had gained him the Tunstall store but little else. He should have known that his justice of the peace and town constable could not match Dolan's district judge and county sheriff. In fact, Martínez's failure to arrest the Tunstall killers lost McSween the initiative and marked a shift toward more aggressive measures. Wilson appointed Dick Brewer a special constable and turned over the warrants to him. At the head of McSween's army, self-anointed as the "Regulators," Brewer set forth on a hunting expedition.[32]

At the same time, as if to ratify his abdication, McSween had to flee for his life. On February 24 he learned that Dolan had left for Mesilla to get new warrants from Judge Bristol for his and Deputy Barrier's arrest. According to the report, Riley had received a letter from Dolan telling him to alert the military at Fort Stanton to aid Brady in the arrest and to have Jesse Evans ready "to do his part" as soon as the soldiers had withdrawn. On February 27, accompanied by the faithful Barrier, McSween headed for the mountains. For ten days the two men hid first at one farmhouse, then at another.[33]

On March 9 McSween and Barrier returned to Lincoln, only to discover new and even more powerful forces arrayed against them. Only hours earlier Samuel B. Axtell, governor of New Mexico, had visited Lincoln. His presence testified to the Santa Fe connections of Dolan and Riley, now strengthened immensely by the direct interest of the most powerful man in the territory. Thomas B. Catron, United States district attorney for New Mexico and the legal and political dynamo generally regarded as head of the Santa Fe Ring, held the mortgage on all their property and naturally did not want to see it endangered.[34]

Chiefly through Catron, with an assist from Rynerson, Dolan captured Governor Axtell. A handsome and clean-shaven man, Axtell had been a better-than-average chief executive. He was also egotistical, easily flattered, and inclined, as one official observed, "to go off 'half-cocked.'"[35] He surely never thought to doubt the Catron-Rynerson version of events in Lincoln County. On March 4 he telegraphed President Rutherford B. Hayes and urged him to order federal troops to take a hand in the conflict. In due course, orders reached Fort Stanton for the garrison to assist the territorial civil officers in enforcing the law.[36]

The governor's three-hour visit to Lincoln on March 9 left the McSween cause in wreckage. Axtell refused to listen to anyone partial to McSween. Worse, he issued a proclamation declaring Squire Wilson to be occupying the office of justice of the peace illegally, naming Judge Bristol the only proper source of legal processes, and designating Sheriff Brady the only proper authority to execute the law. Thereby, in one stroke the governor demolished McSween's legal edifice, invalidating Dick Brewer's commission as special constable as well as the warrants he carried, and dissolving the color of law under which the Regulators operated.[37]

Against this background, as McSween learned next day from Brewer, the Regulators had been making matters even worse. Armed with the Wilson warrants for Tunstall's killers, they had ridden down to the Pecos, where many of the Mathews posse made their homes. On March 6 they seized two of the culprits, Buck Morton and Frank Baker. On March 9, the very day of Axtell's proclamation, Morton, Baker, and William McCloskey, one of Brewer's men known to be friendly to the prisoners, were shot and killed. The Regulators contended that all three died in an escape attempt, but few believed the story.[38]

Still outside the law, McSween had to flee once again. This time, with the conscientious Barrier still at his side, he took refuge at John Chisum's ranch on the Pecos, and here Susan, returning from the East, joined him. Brewer and the Regulators, outlawed by Governor Axtell's proclamation, took to the mountains to avoid arrest for the murder of Morton, Baker, and McCloskey.

While marking time through March, neither side faltered in its commitment to the extinction of the other. The Dolan forces counted not only their own partisans, dependent in one way or another on The House, but also many small stockmen from the Pecos. These men, mainly Texans, believed that their survival depended on smashing John Chisum, which meant smashing his ally McSween. (Most of their herds, of course, had grown from seed stock rustled from Chisum.) For their part, the Regulators were not only adventurers, accustomed to operating at the edges of the law and beyond, but also small farmers and ranchers, some with families, who had been oppressed by The House. The Hispanics among them drew added cause from the large number of Texans in the enemy ranks. In fact, McSween enjoyed great success in attracting nearly the entire Hispanic population to his support.

Fifty miles distant from Lincoln, McSween exerted little influence on the activities of the Regulators until a party visited him at Chisum's ranch near the end of March. What passed between them remains uncertain, but the Regulators rode back to Lincoln resolved to kill Sheriff William Brady. McSween's partisans viewed the sheriff as a prime cause of Tunstall's death. Brady also carried a warrant for McSween's arrest that, if served, would land him in jail and expose him to what he regarded as certain death. In the meeting at Chisum's ranch, McSween may have urged the Regulators to kill the sheriff, and he may even have promised a reward for the deed; or the Regulators, drawing their own conclusions, may have formed such a resolve without McSween's prompting.[39]

If McSween advocated Brady's killing, he not only made a major tactical blunder, one that cost him much public sympathy, but he also stepped out of character. By the end of March, however, he was a truly desperate man, faced with personal and financial ruin. Moreover, Susan had joined him. Made of tougher fiber by far than her mate, she was even more obsessively ambitious for wealth and more ruthless in its quest. As the war grew hotter, she showed herself just as ready as the Regulators to fight back with violence and even homicide. To urge Brady's slaying would not have been out of her character as much as that of her husband.[40]

Whatever McSween's attitude, during the first week of April the Regulators threw away the goodwill of the people. On the morning of April 1 a burst of gunfire from behind the corral wall adjoining the Tunstall store cut down Brady and a deputy. Three days later a party of Regulators had a shoot-out at Blazer's Mills with Andrew L. (Buck-shot) Roberts, one of the men for whom they had warrants issued by Justice Wilson. They killed Roberts, and although Dick Brewer died too, the affair tended to be judged as murder. These killings, especially the ambush of Brady, outraged public opinion; and the report that Brewer and his men had been at Blazer's Mills while en route to assassinate Judge Bristol and District Attorney Rynerson, who were traveling to Lincoln to hold court, alienated still more supporters.[41]

McSween returned to Lincoln on April 1, drawn by an erroneous notice of court convening on this day. He arrived amid the hysteria following Brady's murder, and at once he was arrested, with others of his followers, by one of Brady's deputies. Still fearful of Lincoln's jail, he persuaded the military to hold him at Fort Stanton. There he spent the week, awaiting the opening of court on April 8.

From McSween's standpoint, the proceedings of the district court brought vindication. Although Judge Bristol threw off all judicial de-tachment and lectured the grand jury on the guilt of Alexander McSween, the jurors refused to indict him for embezzlement.

From every other standpoint, the session turned out to be an exercise in confusion and futility. Judge Bristol commuted daily from Fort Stanton under military escort, and soldiers stood by to ensure decorum. No juror or witness could free himself of partisanship, and gunmen of both factions made the atmosphere heavy with intimida-tion. The grand jury returned indictments for the murders of Tunstall, Brady and deputy, and Buckshot Roberts, but it ignored the killing of Morton, Baker, and McCloskey. The indictments, moreover, fell almost indiscriminately on those implicated and omitted men whom everyone knew to be guilty.[42]

Court adjourned on April 24, with McSween the apparent victor. In a burst of good feeling, Lincoln's citizens assembled that evening in a public meeting and adopted resolutions expressing confidence that the county verged on a new era of peace and prosperity. The old feuds would now cease, they predicted, "since the cause has been removed." And so it seemed. Threatened with death by the Regulators, Major Murphy had fled to Fort Stanton in preparation for moving to Santa Fe. There, the following October, he died a hopeless alcoholic. Also, seemingly in surrender, Dolan and Riley had closed their store and soon turned over their mortgaged property to Tom Catron.[43]

McSween had not won. Though badly shaken, Dolan's partisans

had not given up. The Pecos stockmen had not brought down John Chisum. And despite Brewer's death, the Regulators remained an organized body even though many of them had been indicted for murder. They had a new leader, Frank McNab, a former "cattle detective" who had hunted rustlers for big cowmen like Chisum, a background that did nothing to endear him to Chisum's Pecos neighbors. McNab obtained a commission as deputy constable from the justice of the peace of Precinct No. 2 at San Patricio, and so drew another thin covering of legality over the Regulators.[44]

The Regulators made their headquarters at McSween's house, with four or five occupying each of the rooms. There, the new sheriff frequently visited and caroused with them. John Copeland was a hulking man of thirty-seven years, a butcher by trade, who had been appointed sheriff by the county commission on April 10. His mind worked slowly, and he could be influenced easily by almost anyone. McSween readily dominated him. Although he carried warrants for at least five of the Regulators, including Billy Bonney, Copeland seems never to have tried to arrest anyone on the McSween side.[45]

Angered by Copeland's subservience to McSween, Dolan's followers decided that the sheriff needed a posse to help him carry out his duties. After mobilizing the Pecos warriors once again, two of Brady's former deputies advanced on Lincoln with a force of more than twenty men. On April 29, east of Lincoln, they encountered McNab and two Regulators. Opening fire, they killed McNab, mortally wounded one of his men, and captured the other. Next morning they sent word to Copeland that they had come to help him in making arrests. When they reached the edge of town, Copeland and the Regulators answered with gunfire.

The clash of April 30 marked an escalation of the Lincoln County War. From the scattered ambushes and assassinations of guerrilla warfare, the conflict had moved to open battle. Copeland sent for troops, however, and the battle ended without further bloodshed. Fearing to provoke the army, the entire band from the Pecos surrendered on the promise of the detachment commander not to turn them over to Copeland and the Regulators.[46]

The affair now took on comic opera overtones. McSween wrote out a warrant for the arrest of eighteen of these men for the murder of McNab, hastened to San Patricio to obtain the signature of the justice of the peace of Precinct No. 2, and had Copeland take it to

Fort Stanton. Meanwhile, two of the men held at Fort Stanton swore an affidavit charging the Regulators with riot. A courier hurried over to Blazer's Mills and, on the basis of the affidavit, obtained a warrant from the justice of the peace of Precinct No. 3 for the arrest of McSween and some twenty of his men. The new commanding officer at the fort, Lieutenant Colonel Nathan A. M. Dudley, lectured Copeland on his duty to enforce the law impartially, handed him the warrant, and sent him off with a posse of soldiers to round up McSween and his followers. With nearly thirty men in military custody and the number rising, Copeland now became confused, and on the evening of May 4 he turned everyone loose with the injunction to go home and quit feuding. "Both parties seem to have had a scare," Dudley observed dryly.[47]

By this time, with the bravos of both sides dashing about the country looking for a fight, neither Dolan nor McSween had much influence on events. Possibly goaded by Susan, McSween tried to overcome his instincts and go along with the activities of the rowdies who rode in his cause. Widenmann, ever the blusterer, gloried in the role of swaggering gunslinger. Colonel Dudley observed him and a companion strutting about Fort Stanton like "walking Gatling guns," and a farmer told how Widenmann had so often threatened him with death if he did not join the McSween forces that he finally abandoned his farm and fled the county.[48]

For his part, Dolan appeared to have left the field altogether, though hardly in abject surrender. Early in May he helped Murphy move to Santa Fe and remained there for a month. Besides writing self-serving letters to the *New Mexican,* he busied himself in further plots with Governor Axtell. The law required Sheriff Copeland to post bond as tax collector within thirty days of his appointment. Because the tax lists needed to fix the amount of the bond had not been made out, he failed to meet the deadline. The governor moved swiftly. On May 28 he issued still another proclamation, removing Copeland as sheriff and appointing a Brady deputy, George W. Peppin, as successor. The proclamation also commanded all armed men to disband, return to their homes, and not act as posse members so long as U.S. soldiers could be summoned. In other words, only soldiers could serve in posses, and they only under the control of the new sheriff.[49]

Two days after the proclamation, word reached Santa Fe of another foolish move by the Regulators. Two weeks earlier, under a transparent legal pretext, they had raided the Dolan cow camp on the Pecos, killed a herder, scattered the herd, and run off with twenty-five horses and two mules. The stock, however, no longer belonged to Dolan but to Tom Catron. When Catron learned of the fate of his cattle on May 30, he promptly went to Governor Axtell. The governor, in turn, requested Colonel Edward Hatch, U.S. Army commander in New Mexico, to send troops to the Pecos to protect Catron's interests and to disarm all groups ranging that area. Hatch helpfully complied, but his superiors told him that he had overstepped his authority, and he called off the operation.[50]

While Dolan looked to Axtell, Catron, and other high officials for aid, the McSween people were not wholly without influential friends. Rob Widenmann had ties to Interior Secretary Carl Schurz. The Reverend Taylor F. Ealy, a Presbyterian clergyman imported by McSween to elevate the community, wrote letters to an uncle who sat in the House of Representatives. An English friend of President Hayes, Montague R. Leverson, took up the McSween cause and wrote wordy letters denouncing Axtell, Catron, and the military authorities at Fort Stanton. Most decisively, the British minister in Washington demanded an investigation of the killing of a British subject. As a result of all this fuss, the federal government embarked on an inquiry into the Lincoln County troubles. In May and June, Frank Warner Angel, agent for the Departments of Justice and the Interior, took testimony in Lincoln, Fort Stanton, and Mesilla. Although he seemed to sympathize with the McSween cause, his report would come too late to save the embattled lawyer.[51]

"Dad" Peppin qualified for his appointment as sheriff in Mesilla in mid-June. A stonemason by trade, and thirty-nine years old, he was no better equipped than Copeland, whom he resembled in amiability, good intentions, and weakness of intellect. Like Copeland, too, he was easily led, and he followed Dolan as readily as Copeland had followed McSween.

Even before Peppin reached Lincoln on June 18, McSween and his men learned to their consternation that he brought from Mesilla more than his commissions as sheriff and deputy U.S. marshal. He carried with him United States warrants for the arrest of nine Regulators involved in the killing of Buckshot Roberts, with the rationale being that Blazer's Mills lay within the Indian reservation and thus came under federal jurisdiction. Peppin also brought a formidable army to serve the warrants. In violation of the governor's ban on citizen posses, he had not only the usual collection of Dolan henchmen and Pecos warriors but a gang of eleven outlaws headed by John Kinney, a ruffian and stock thief from the Río Grande even more notorious than Jesse Evans.[52] To back up his posse, the sheriff obtained a detachment of soldiers from Colonel Dudley at Fort Stanton. And finally, accompanying Peppin, Jimmy Dolan came home. Unwilling to face this array, the Regulators hastily abandoned Lincoln and fled to the mountains.[53]

Although no warrants stood against him, McSween took the field with his army—afoot, "clean shaved and with a very large hat."[54] His talents did not run to field soldiering, and although he may have departed from habit to buckle on a gun, he surely did not command. That role fell to Josiah G. (Doc) Scurlock, who had been elected captain after the slaying of McNab. McSween and the Regulators hid in the mountains around San Patricio, a tiny adobe village on the Río Ruidoso just above its junction with the Río Bonito, and they often came into town. It was a congenial place, whose almost completely Hispanic population favored the McSween cause and contributed about a dozen gunmen to the Regulator ranks.

The war now grew deadlier. On June 27 and again on July 3, Peppin posses energized by Jimmy Dolan and John Kinney struck at San Patricio and vicinity, and the two forces exchanged gunfire. No one was badly hurt, but a wounded horse furnished a pretext for counting McSween among the wanted men. Anyone's bullet might have hit the horse, but McSween was charged with assault with intent to kill. Ironically, the warrant was issued from the court of Squire Wilson, who was once again, thanks to a special election, justice of the peace of Precinct No. 1. After the clash of July 3, the Regulators rode down to Chisum's ranch, where on Independence Day another skirmish took place.[55]

As the war gathered momentum, the army suddenly ceased to exert a moderating influence or to play any role at all. For reasons that had little to do with the turmoil in New Mexico, Congress had attached a rider to the army appropriations act prohibiting the use of federal troops in civil disturbances. Colonel Dudley gave notice that his soldiers could no longer participate in any way in the civil troubles of Lincoln County.[56]

With the army no longer at Peppin's call, McSween's strategists saw a chance to regain the initiative. After assembling a force of about sixty fighters, they reoccupied Lincoln on July 14, dividing themselves among the McSween house and other buildings. The next day Peppin possemen numbering about forty took up a station in Sam Wortley's hotel. The stage was set for the conflict soon to be known as the "Five-Day Battle."[57]

The McSween forces enjoyed every prospect of victory. On the climactic day, however, they lost their advantages. Colonel Dudley, with five officers and thirty-five soldiers, marched into Lincoln and camped in the middle of town. They came solely, as Dudley made clear, to protect women and children, and they generally pursued a course of neutrality. But their presence neutralized most of McSween's defenders and soon flushed them out of town, leaving only the handful in the McSween house and Tunstall store. Emboldened, Peppin's posse, including the Pecos warriors and Kinney's gangsters, closed in on this last bastion of the Regulators.

Inside, Alexander McSween confronted his fate with resignation. Ever since Peppin's return from Mesilla, he had given way to despair, tossed about on the whims of the Regulators, and awaiting the inevitable denouement. "I saw McSween just a month before he was killed," recalled a close friend. "He seemed to think he was doomed."[58] His widow later confirmed her husband's lethargic mood to a would-be chronicler of the Lincoln County War, and she explained to another that McSween had done many things he regretted because of the "foolhardy boys" with whom he rode.[59] He was indeed doomed. Throughout the afternoon, flames kindled by the attackers ate away at room after room. By nightfall, only one remained. The defenders made a break for it. Five bullets riddled McSween, and he fell on his back doorstep.

McSween's death marked the close of the first stage of the Lincoln County War—the struggle to determine whether an existing monopoly or an aspiring monopoly would dominate Lincoln County. Neither, it turned out, would achieve that distinction, for both collapsed in the rubble of war.

But the war did not end. Even before the Five-Day Battle, it had taken on a life of its own, quite independent of its leaders. By the April term of court, the entire citizenry had become polarized. Almost everyone chose sides, some for reasons of personal friendship or private gain, and others because they had been threatened with harm if they did not. The combatants pushed the fight with fervor, even as their leaders showed signs of weakening. They fought not alone for money and plunder, but also because they had convinced themselves of the justice of their cause. All rationalized that they fought in the service of lawful institutions—for public purposes that happened also to serve private purposes. As McSween and perhaps even Dolan wavered in their resolve, the armies simply overran their leaders. "They have created a storm they cannot control," editorialized the *Independent* early in May.[60]

The second phase of the Lincoln County War opened almost at once. No longer a contest between opposing commercial barons, it now became a desperate battle against outlaws who converged from other parts of the West. In part they came because of the withdrawal of the army from civil affairs, but they came too because of the breakdown of the institutions of law and the demoralization of the population. McSween had contributed substantially to the last two conditions, and so his ghost hovered over the remainder of the Lincoln County War.

Of all the principal figures in these events, McSween remains the most elusive, the one hardest to understand. To his friends and followers, he projected the image of an honorable, ethical, and highly moral and religious man, one always deeply concerned about fairness and justice in human relations. He impressed his enemies, on the other hand, as a scheming, tricky, underhanded, and unscrupulous lawyer, as heedless of human life as those he fought. This portrait drew substance from McSween's complicity in Tunstall's schemes and his role in the conflict set off by Tunstall's death, which betrayed a hunger for wealth, power, and stature that was at odds with his professed sense of right and decency. Possibly his complex makeup masked a struggle between both persona, a struggle that gained its ultimate resolution only on the back doorstep of his blazing home.

2
Billy
the Kid

As Alexander McSween died on the back doorstep of his blazing home, Billy the Kid made good his escape. The fire had eaten from room to room, finally leaving the defenders with the choice of burning, surrendering, or making a break for it. From the kitchen door they burst into the night, lit by the flames of the burning house. The posse's fire drove part of them back, McSween included. But, dodging bullets, the Kid and several companions raced across the opening between the McSween house and the Tunstall store, veered to the north, and lost themselves in the trees along the Río Bonito. Ten minutes later, on this night of July 19, 1878, a burst of gunfire killed Alexander McSween.[1]

Billy the Kid emerged from the flaming wreckage of McSween's home as a minor celebrity, known throughout New Mexico Territory as a prominent fighter in the Lincoln County War and an outlaw wanted on charges originating in the war. Even at the war's end, however, he had not become known as Billy the Kid, and the exciting adventures that traced his path from Lincoln County to the pistol flash that ended his brief career in a darkened bedroom at Fort Sumner hardly account for the towering stature he later attained in American folklore. The explanation for that phenomenon lies more in the dynamics of mythmaking than in the reality of his life. The legend, however, gives global significance to a life that is otherwise of interest to only a handful of antiquarians. Because of the legend, the life invites careful scrutiny, to discover if it can be compressed into its true human dimensions.[2]

He came to Lincoln County late in October 1877, a few weeks

after his eighteenth birthday and thus hardly out of adolescence. He looked his youth—140 pounds, spare, of medium stature, with brown hair, light complexion, and a smooth face betraying the downy beginnings of a beard and mustache. Two squirrel-like front teeth slightly marred his appearance. He rode well and shot well and practiced all the time. With agreeable and winning ways, he made friends easily, especially with the Hispanics, whose language he spoke fluently.[3] He was basically a scrappy tough, seasoned by the raw life of the Silver City mining camp. He had killed at least one man, a bully at Fort Grant, Arizona, whose death could not be properly judged premeditated or cold-blooded. Like many another drifter, he gave a false name, William H. Bonney; but he also took his stepfather's surname and answered to Henry Antrim, Kid Antrim, or just Kid.

Billy Bonney arrived in Lincoln County as a fugitive from the Arizona murder charge. He came by way of Mesilla, where he probably spent a few weeks with Jesse Evans's gang of horse thieves, known as The Boys. He then crossed the rugged Guadalupe Mountains to the lower Pecos and from there made his way back to the high country of the Sierra Blanca. On the upper Peñasco he fell in with a band of some thirty gunmen and, on November 17, 1877, helped them break Jesse Evans and three of his gang out of the Lincoln jail. Toward the end of November he hired on as a cowhand at the newly acquired cattle ranch of John H. Tunstall on the Río Félix.[4]

The ranch on the Río Félix was but one of the enterprises the young Englishman had launched, with lawyer Alexander McSween and others, in an effort to make a fortune through the monopoly control of Lincoln County's economy. Success required the destruction of the existing monopoly of James J. Dolan and John H. Riley, who had succeeded to the commercial empire, known simply as The House, erected by Lawrence G. Murphy. The struggle between the rival groups held the makings of the Lincoln County War. When Bonney went to work for John H. Tunstall late in 1877, commercial competition verged on violent confrontation.

In the few weeks before the slaying of Tunstall touched off the Lincoln County War, Bonney had little chance to form the fast friendship of legend with his employer. The store in Lincoln and other concerns kept Tunstall away from the ranch most of this time. To his family in England, Tunstall described in detail another hand, John Middleton, a tough-looking cowboy who handled rifle and pistol with superlative skill, but not once did he mention Bonney. The Kid may have liked and admired the ranch owner, but it had to be from some distance.[5]

Bonney's friends, rather, were his daily companions—Middleton; Richard Brewer, the ranch foreman, who probably recruited him; Godfrey Gauss, the gentle, fatherly old cook; and especially Fred Waite. Six years older, a Choctaw from the Indian Territory, Waite became Billy's constant companion. At winter's end, the two planned to begin farming their own spread on the Peñasco. Instead, war broke out.[6]

The conflict found its immediate stimulus in the courts. Judge Warren Bristol and Prosecuting Attorney William L. Rynerson favored the Dolan cause, as did Sheriff William Brady, a steadfast, conscientious lawman who nonetheless had ties to The House. In McSween's questionable handling of the assets of an estate, Dolan saw pretext to invoke the law against McSween. He manipulated the heirs to the estate into having the lawyer arrested on an embezzlement charge and also into bringing civil suit against him for ten thousand dollars in damages. As security against this sum, Judge Bristol issued a writ for the attachment of McSween's property.

These maneuvers brought the opening scenes of the war to the very doorstep of Bonney and his friend. They were at the Tunstall ranch on February 13, 1878, when Deputy Jacob B. Mathews and a posse of four rode up with orders from Sheriff Brady to impound Tunstall's cattle. On the erroneous though understandable theory that a business partnership made Tunstall's property partly McSween's, Brady had already attached the entire contents of the Tunstall store in Lincoln. Now he planned to attach Tunstall's stock on the Félix. Brewer said that he could have any McSween cows he could find but must leave Tunstall's alone. Bonney and his friends stood by with arms ready to back up their foreman, so Mathews rode back to Lincoln for new instructions.

Five days later he tried again, this time with a posse of more than twenty men. But Tunstall had taken the measure of his adversary and had decided that only by giving in could bloodshed be averted. He hurried to the ranch and took charge. Leaving Gauss to surrender the cattle to the posse, he and the other hands left for Lincoln early on the morning of February 18. Waite drove a wagon on the road, while Bonney, Brewer, Middleton, and Tunstall's aide Rob Widenmann joined their chief to herd nine horses along the shorter trail through the mountains. Late that afternoon, as Bonney and Middleton lagged behind the rest, a dozen or more horseman stormed up the trail in their rear, firing, shouting, and spurring their mounts at the gallop. While Middleton rushed to find Tunstall, Bonney made for a wooded hilltop that offered defensive cover. Here he joined Brewer and Widenmann, who had left the trail in pursuit of some wild turkeys. Middleton soon rode up, but Tunstall had tarried on the trail. From beyond an intervening hill came the sound of gunfire. "They've killed Tunstall," said Middleton.

Tunstall had fallen before a subposse headed by William S. (Buck) Morton. Mathews had sent this group to overtake Tunstall and seize the horses. Only two men were with Morton in the final confrontation with Tunstall, outlaw chief Jesse Evans and one of his gang, Tom Hill. They had joined the posse on the pretext of recovering a horse they had lent to Bonney. The official version was that Tunstall resisted arrest and had to be killed. No one on either side could dispute the explanation from direct observation, but none of Tunstall's friends believed it.[7]

Tunstall's killing started Billy the Kid on the road to notoriety. Whether to avenge his employer's slaying or from other motives, he rose swiftly to prominence among the men who rallied to the standard of Alexander McSween. Such a force, between thirty and fifty strong, began gathering at McSween's home on the night of February 18, even before word came of Tunstall's death. In addition to Brewer, Bonney, Waite, and Middleton, there were other cowhands well acquainted with guns and willing to dedicate them to the McSween cause. There were also outraged citizens who had long resented the tyranny of The House.

In the confused maneuvers of the next few days, these men emerged as a key element of McSween's strategy. As Dolan had his judge, so McSween sought one of his own—bumbling old John B. Wilson, justice of the peace of Precinct No. 1. And as Dolan had his posse riding behind the badge of Sheriff Brady, McSween sought one of his own—Bonney and the other gunmen gathered in his home, operating under the authority of Atanacio Martínez, constable of Precinct No. 1. When Martínez balked at the role prescribed for him, Bonney stepped forward with a blunt threat to do as he was told or be killed.[8]

For nearly a week these two legally constituted posses, armed with legally issued warrants for a multitude of arrests, sparred with each other. On one especially tense day, only the presence of soldiers from Fort Stanton prevented a gun fight between the two groups. In each confrontation Bonney stood out among the most aggressive of the Martínez posse. In the end McSween's stratagem failed. District Attorney Rynerson refused to accept McSween's bond, and Judge Bristol wrote out a new warrant for the lawyer's arrest. Certain that he would be killed if clapped in Sheriff Brady's jail, McSween fled Lincoln.[9]

The Martínez posse contained the beginnings of the fighting force that called itself the Regulators. Although they professed to be above the partisanship of McSween and Dolan, for the next five months they fought McSween's battle. Like Dolan's warriors, they rode under color of the law. Their captain, Dick Brewer, bore a commission as special constable from Justice of the Peace Wilson and carried the warrant issued from his court for the arrest of Tunstall's killers.

About a dozen men, all Anglo, formed the core group of the Regulators and figured in almost all of their operations from the maneuvers of late February to the shootout at McSween's home in July. On occasion other men, both Anglo and Hispanic, swelled the ranks to twenty and even thirty. In the final battle for Lincoln, they numbered more than sixty.

As one of this core group of Regulators, Bonney achieved his significance in the first stage of the Lincoln County War. He took part in every major incident, sometimes with more visibility than his companions and sometimes with less. Rarely a leader, he was always the diligent, active soldier. At age eighteen essentially an unformed personality, he may well have taken on his adult makeup and values from the older men with whom he shared the hardships and dangers of 1878.[10]

These men were not merely hired guns. Enemies accused McSween of paying each Regulator four dollars a day. Actually, while holding forth the prospect of reward from the purse of the elder Tunstall in London, McSween paid only for their food and other supplies. Therefore, the Regulators fought in the hope of ultimate gain and because they wanted to break the grip of The House on their daily lives. They were as lawless and violent as Dolan's fighters, as given to settling disputes with a Winchester or Colt, and as prone to supplementing their income with occasional larceny. But also like Dolan's men, they were farmers, stockmen, or laborers who spent most of their time in honest toil. From such men did Billy Bonney absorb his outlook on life.[11]

The first Regulator mission that Bonney joined was the search for Buck Morton, who had headed the subposse that killed Tunstall. Morton had charge of Dolan's cow camp at Seven Rivers, on the lower Pecos. Near there, on March 6, Brewer and ten Regulators flushed Morton and Frank Baker, a Jesse Evans henchman who had also been with Morton's subposse. Brewer and his men had hoped that they would not have to take the fugitives alive, but after a long and tiring chase they surrendered. In Roswell, Morton posted a letter to a friend in Virginia predicting his and Baker's death before they could reach Lincoln.

And in fact they and William McCloskey, a former Tunstall employee who had attached himself to the party, never reached Lincoln. As Brewer explained to McSween, on March 9 Morton had grabbed McCloskey's pistol and shot him, and then with Baker had made a break for safety, only to be gunned down by the Regulators. No participant ever admitted to another version, but scarcely anyone else believed that the three men had not been simply executed. McCloskey, a friend of Morton and not a Regulator, could not be trusted to stick to the official explanation and thus had to be dispatched along with the other victims. The bodies of Morton and Baker, according to report, each contained eleven bullets, one for each Regulator.[12]

Billy loomed large in the next action of the Regulators. After meeting with McSween at John Chisum's ranch late in March, Bonney and five others laid plans to remove one of the major instruments of McSween's ballooning troubles with the law: Sheriff William Brady. On the night of March 31 they slipped into the corral behind the Tunstall store. An adobe wall with a gate projecting eastward from the rear of the building hid them from the street. About midmorning on April 1, Sheriff Brady, with deputies George Hindman, Jacob Mathews, George Peppin, and John Long, walked down the street.

As the officers passed the wall, the men behind it loosed a fusillade of rifle fire. Brady fell, riddled by as many as a dozen bullets, Hindman with one. Crying for water, Hindman tried to rise. Ike Stockton, who kept a saloon nearby, dashed out to help, but Hindman died. The other deputies had run to the safety of a house across the street. Bonney and Jim French sprinted from the corral into the street and stooped over Brady, possibly to search his pockets for the McSween arrest warrant. From their refuge, Mathews and his companions opened fire. The Kid picked up Brady's Winchester but was struck in the thigh by a slug, which went through him and hit French in the thigh too. Billy dropped the rifle, and the two ran back to safety.[13]

Bonney's wound did not disable him, but French could not ride. While Bonney and the other Regulators lost themselves in the timber along the Río Bonito, French hobbled to the backdoor of the McSween house, where the Reverend Dr. Taylor F. Ealy and his family were living in McSween's absence. A physician as well as Presbyterian clergyman, Ealy ran a silk handkerchief through the wound and turned French over to Sam Corbet, a meek little fellow who had clerked in the Tunstall store. Corbet hid French somewhere—under the floor, Ealy said, with two pistols clutched in his hands—and the posse that tracked the blood to the backdoor and searched the house three times failed to find him. That night, the Kid stole back and rescued his friend.[14]

Bonney and French must not have had serious wounds, for on April 4 they appeared with Brewer and eleven other Regulators at South Fork, the location of Blazer's Mills and the Mescalero Apache Indian Agency. As they ate lunch at the home of the Indian agent, Andrew L. (Buckshot) Roberts rode up on his mule. A small-time stockman from the Ruidoso, he had formerly worked at Dolan's South Fork store and had close friends in the tiny community. He had also ridden with the Mathews posse that had killed Tunstall, and Brewer had his name on the warrant from Justice Wilson.

Roberts was a tough scrapper, and not easily intimidated. Before the others came out of the house, Frank Coe took him around to a side porch and tried to persuade him to surrender, but he refused. Soon part of the men appeared, and firing at once erupted. Charlie Bowdre put a bullet into Roberts's groin, but the game little fighter, despite a bad arm, worked his Winchester carbine with deadly effect. One bullet tore off Bowdre's gun belt, another hit Middleton in the chest, and still another smashed the stock of George Coe's rifle and mangled his trigger finger. As the Regulators backed off, Roberts struggled through a doorway, dragged a mattress from a bed, and barricaded himself for defense. Bonney had not been with the party that had first confronted Roberts. Now, according to Frank Coe, "The Kid slipped in between the wall and a wagon. Roberts took a shot at him, just shaved his arm. Kid backed out as it was too hot there for him."

Circling through a corral and down the creek, Brewer posted himself behind a stack of logs about a hundred yards from the doorway. Roberts glimpsed the puff of smoke from Brewer's first shot. When Brewer rose for a second shot, Roberts sent a bullet through his brain. That cooled the ardor of the Regulators, and they pulled out, leaving Roberts to linger painfully through the night before dying.[15]

After Blazer's Mills, the Regulators lay low through April. The cold-blooded assassination of Brady and Hindman, followed by the killing of Roberts, alienated much of the public sympathy they had enjoyed. To make matters worse, rumors circulated that they had been at Blazer's Mills as part of a plot to ambush Judge Bristol and District Attorney Rynerson, en route from Mesilla to hold the April term of court in Lincoln. The court then dealt a further blow. Although exonerating McSween of embezzlement and generally favoring his cause, the grand jury indicted Bonney, Middleton, and Henry Brown for the murder of Sheriff Brady, and Bowdre for the murder of Roberts.[16]

No sooner had court adjourned than hostilities resumed with fresh vigor. McSween, now free of the embezzlement charge, returned to his home in Lincoln and gathered about him a force of Regulators, including Bonney and the others under indictment for murder. The new sheriff, John Copeland, turned out to be a McSween partisan. He spent much time with the gunmen in the McSween house but made no move to serve the arrest warrants he carried in his pocket. A band of Dolan's friends, about thirty stockmen from the lower Pecos under William H. Johnson, decided to ride up to Lincoln and help Copeland arrest Bonney, Middleton, Brown, and Bowdre. On the way they encountered Frank McNab, Brewer's successor as Regulator chief, Frank Coe, and Ab Saunders, Coe's brother-in-law. In the ensuing shootout, McNab was killed, Saunders received a mortal wound, and Coe fell captive.

Early the next morning, April 30, the Johnson gunmen approached Lincoln. Part of them circled the town and took station in the Dolan store, now closed in bankruptcy. The rest spread out in the timber along the river opposite the Isaac Ellis store on the eastern edge of town. The Battle of Lincoln opened as George Coe fired from the roof of the Ellis store and shattered the ankles of "Dutch Charlie" Kruling. The men in the Dolan store rushed out and headed down the street toward Ellis's store, but McSween's fighters had posted themselves on other rooftops and behind walls and laid down a hot fire. The attackers veered off to the north, crossed the river, and soon united with their confederates downstream. For four hours the two sides exchanged fire without damaging anyone. Early in the afternoon a detachment of black cavalry arrived in response to a request from Sheriff Copeland. They intervened, received the surrender of the Dolan forces, and escorted them to Fort Stanton under arrest.[17]

Billy Bonney did not stand out among the defenders of Lincoln. Presumably, he simply fired at the Dolanites from a rooftop. With Bowdre, Middleton, and others, he then left Lincoln, thus escaping the welter of arrests on both sides that followed. On the evening of May 2, the Kid and his friends were in San Patricio, where McSween bought dinner for them at Dow's store. Shortly after they left for the mountains, a military patrol rode into town and placed McSween under arrest.[18]

No one remained in military custody for long, thanks to the confused and baffling actions of Sheriff Copeland. By May 4 he had released all of the Dolanites and shepherded the McSween people back to Lincoln, where they too went free.

With McNab dead, the Regulators elected their third captain, Josiah G. (Doc) Scurlock. A stockman from the Ruidoso, Doc was a devoted family man and a sensitive intellectual with some medical training in his background. He was also a ruthless killer, as faithful as Bonney in his devotion to the Regulators.[19] He called together Bonney and about ten of the usual crowd and, bolstered by an equal number of Hispanics under Josefita Chaves, headed for the Pecos. He carried the warrants, by now well worn, issued by Justice Wilson in February for the arrest of Tunstall's killers.

On May 14 the Regulator force fell on the Dolan cow camp near Seven Rivers. They drove off the herders, scattered the herd, and seized twenty-five horses and two mules. They also captured the cook, known simply as "Indian." He had been in the posse that killed Tunstall and also figured in the slaying of McNab. Under the usual cloak of attempted escape, the Regulators killed him, with the Kid and Chaves acting as the executioners.[20]

After their May expedition, Scurlock, Bonney, and the other Regulators gathered again in Lincoln, where they operated out of McSween's home. Early in June some of them swore depositions before Justice Wilson for incorporation in the report of government investigator Frank Warner Angel. The Kid's deposition, signed on June 8, dealt mostly with the killing of Tunstall. It was in Rob Widenmann's hand and mirrored his own deposition faithfully enough to suggest that Billy merely signed what had been prepared for him.

With Dolan in Santa Fe and many of the principals in the conflict in Mesilla for another session of district court, much of June was quiet. It was the calm before the storm, for New Mexico Governor Samuel B. Axtell had fired Copeland and appointed a new sheriff, George W. Peppin, who turned out to be as much Dolan's tool as Copeland had been McSween's tool. On June 18 Peppin arrived in Lincoln accompanied by Dolan and a small army of possemen. He also carried newly issued federal warrants for Bonney and the other Regulators involved in the Blazer's Mills fight, with the rationale for federal jurisdiction being that Roberts had been killed on an Indian reservation.[21]

With the odds changed dramatically, Scurlock and his men fled Lincoln rather than face Peppin's guns. McSween accompanied them, although no warrant stood against him. George Washington, Lincoln's ubiquitous black handyman, went along as cook. Hiding in the mountains behind San Patricio, they made the little village their headquarters and took their meals there.

Peppin did not delay in moving against San Patricio. He commanded not only Dolan with his coterie and some of the Pecos warriors, but a band of eleven outlaws from the Río Grande under the notorious John Kinney. At daybreak on June 27 this gang, under Deputy John Long, appeared in the San Patricio plaza. The fugitives were still in the hills, but the posse scooped up George Washington, who promptly spilled out everything he knew about the Regulators. Leaving Kinney and his followers in town, Long took five men up the Ruidoso Valley to check out Newcomb's ranch. While returning, they spied horsemen across the river and, supposing them to be Kinney's party, turned in their direction. A burst of gunfire at seventy-five yards greeted Long's force and dropped two horses, including his own. The enemy wheeled and galloped into the bordering hills.

Long had flushed the Regulators, eleven strong. In addition to Scurlock, Bonney, Bowdre, French, and the other familiar figures, the party included McSween and the ex-sheriff Copeland, together with three Hispanics. The firing brought Kinney at the gallop, so Scurlock and his men scampered up a mountain and deployed for defense. Kinney tried to take the position, but could not get close enough without dangerously exposing his force. Long dispatched a courier for help, and Peppin sent to Fort Stanton for a military posse. A company of black cavalrymen reached the scene late in the afternoon, but the Regulators had pulled out. The troopers followed the trail through the mountains until, early on June 29, a messenger recalled them to Fort Stanton.[22]

Peppin tried again on July 3. Cleverly, he organized a posse of fifteen Hispanics under José Chaves y Baca. McSween had won Hispanics to his standard, and Peppin intended to play the same game, although at least one man hinted that he had been coerced into serving.

This time the Regulators were not in the hills, but posted on the rooftops of San Patricio. Riding into the plaza at daybreak, the attackers ran into a storm of bullets that drove them hastily back out of range, with one man dragging a smashed arm. They sent for help, but by the time Long arrived with Dolan, Kinney, and reinforcements, the fugitives had flown. The posse followed, but four miles east of town they confronted Scurlock and his men deployed along the crest of a ridge. A well-aimed volley from the heights downed two horses and sent the pursuers hurrying back to San Patricio. There, ostensibly searching for more Regulators, they ransacked the town and terrorized the inhabitants so thoroughly that a delegation of twenty-seven women trekked to Fort Stanton to appeal for military protection.[23]

After the fight at San Patricio, the Regulators continued down the Río Hondo to Chisum's ranch. "We went down to visit Old John and to rest on the Fourth," recalled George Coe. It was not a restful Independence Day. While the ranch hands prepared a big dinner, the Coes, Bonney, and others rode over to Ash Upson's store to buy candy for Chisum's niece. On the return a posse jumped them, and the two sides exchanged shots in a running fight back to the ranch. The posse kept the ranch buildings under long-range siege all day, but that night they gave up and departed.[24]

Once more the odds shifted to the McSween side. The recall of the posse of soldiers from the Regulator trail on June 29 marked an abrupt change in military policy. Congress had imposed a ban on all military aid to civil authorities in enforcing the law. Suddenly, Peppin could no longer look to Fort Stanton for help. Resolved on a showdown, the Regulators hastened back to Lincoln, gathering strength along the way. On July 14, more than sixty strong, they reoccupied the town. With the arrival of some thirty to forty Peppin possemen—

Dolan henchmen, Pecos warriors, Kinney's outlaws, and even bandit chief Jesse Evans—the stage was set for the so-called Five-Day Battle.[25]

McSween's forces enjoyed the advantage not only of strength but of position. Part of the men held the Ellis store on the eastern edge of town, part the Montaño store in the center of town, and the balance the Tunstall store and McSween house near the western edge of town. The Peppin forces, based in Sam Wortley's hotel just west of the McSween house, could do little but snipe from cover at these positions. Any attempt to seize them would cost heavy casualties.

Billy Bonney joined McSween and his wife Susan in their home, one among fourteen gunmen who held this position. Hispanics recently recruited to the cause composed most of the force. Besides Bonney, only two were hardcore Regulators, Jim French and Tom O'Folliard, a young fellow who had come up from Texas in June and formed a worshipful friendship with the Kid. Through the rising tension and sporadic gunfire of the next five days, McSween grew more and more despondent. By the last day, as Susan remembered, "The Kid was lively and McSween was sad. McSween sat with his head down, and the Kid shook him and told him to get up."[26]

The Regulators made two tactical errors that were to have fatal consequences. On July 16 the men in the McSween house spied a horseman coming from the west, with the setting sun at his back. They fired, and his horse, taking fright, threw him. Remounting, the rider galloped to the safety of the Wortley Hotel. The man turned out to be a trooper from Fort Stanton bringing Peppin word that he could not have the cannon he had asked for.

Next day, some officers came to town to investigate this incident. When they were told that a posse member lay badly wounded within range of the Montaño store, the surgeon and another officer went to give succor. Gunfire from the store sent bullets singing over their heads. They brought back the man, who later died, but the spectacle of McSween riflemen firing at U.S. soldiers did nothing to endear his cause to the military authorities.[27]

These events, coupled with continuing appeals for military help from Lincoln citizens, tipped the balance at Fort Stanton. Lieutenant Colonel Nathan A. M. Dudley and his officers reasoned that, while they could not aid Peppin as they wanted, no one could object to their presence in Lincoln for the purely humanitarian purpose of protecting women and children. On the morning of July 19, they marched into Lincoln with thirty-five soldiers, let everyone know why they had come, and served notice that any bullets flying their way would earn serious consequences for the people who fired them.[28]

Dudley's presence in Lincoln threw the advantage back to Peppin. It caused the McSween forces to evacuate the Montaño and Ellis stores and withdraw to the north side of the Río Bonito, where they could not influence events in town. It thus left the defenders of the McSween house and Tunstall store to shift for themselves, and it emboldened Peppin's men to close in for the kill. Despite the vigorous appeals of Susan McSween, Dudley refused high-mindedly to intervene to save her beleaguered husband and his protectors. Early in the afternoon, the posse succeeded in firing the house, and by dark the occupants had to risk the dash for safety. The Kid, O'Folliard, French, and others made it. McSween did not. As two lay dead or dying in the rubble of his home, "the big killing," as one participant called it, cut down the lawyer and three others in his backyard.

McSween's death, removing one of the two principal adversaries, ended the first stage of the Lincoln County War and opened the second. Now, however, it could hardly be termed war, for no longer did two forces contend for victory. Instead, the Regulators and Peppin's posse fragmented and scattered over the county to plunder and, when necessary, kill and destroy. With the army neutralized and Peppin afraid to venture beyond sight of Fort Stanton, desperadoes rushed from elsewhere to take advantage of the absence of any authority to uphold law and order. Citizens cowered in their homes or abandoned them altogether.

The last action in which the Regulators engaged as a body took place at the Indian agency on August 5. Their motives are obscure. One report had them traveling en route to recover stolen stock. The agent, Frederick C. Godfroy, felt certain that they meant to kill him. Frank Coe explained, unconvincingly, that they wanted to visit the grave of Dick Brewer, who had been buried at the agency after the Blazer's Mills fight of April 4. Most likely, they went to steal ponies belonging to the Indians.

Approaching the agency, the Kid and others of the Anglo contingent paused to drink from a spring. The Hispanics continued and soon encountered a party of Indians. Firing broke out. Beyond, Godfroy and his clerk, Morris Bernstein, were issuing rations to some

Indian women. Bernstein hastily mounted and galloped out to investigate. He promptly got caught up in the gun battle and was shot down by Atanacio Martínez, the Lincoln constable who had occasionally ridden with the Regulators since the first hostilities in February. Godfroy and a few soldiers who happened to be at the agency sprang to the defense. The confused firing that followed killed the Kid's horse, and he escaped injury only by mounting behind George Coe and galloping across an open glade under heavy fire. The Anglo group circled the agency to the corral and made off with all the horses and mules. Godfroy found Bernstein's body lying face down, with four bullet holes in it. His pockets had been emptied and his rifle and pistol taken.[29]

The theft of government stock gave Colonel Dudley the excuse to put a detachment of troopers on the trail of the culprits, but they scattered and easily escaped. For the next few months the Kid, with the faithful O'Folliard at his side, bounced back and forth between Fort Sumner and Lincoln. Others among the Regulators did the same, although Waite, Middleton, and Brown left New Mexico for good. On September 6 the Kid and others stole fifteen horses from Charles Fritz's ranch, east of Lincoln, and added them to a herd that they eventually disposed of in the Texas panhandle.[30]

Billy Bonney, increasingly the open outlaw rather than the defender of a cause claiming a semblance of legality, added his full measure to the disorders that afflicted Lincoln County throughout the last half of 1878, but others more than matched his contribution. The Kinney and Evans gangs had their fling, as did the Pecos warriors, and between them and the roving squads of Regulators the explosive bitterness of the Dolan-McSween feud persisted. But the most vicious scourge of the county had nothing to do with old rivalries. This was John Selman's "Wrestlers"—a term of obscure origin doubtless corrupted from "rustler." Like the others, they stole; but unlike the others, they killed, senselessly and indiscriminately and with no apparent motive, and they brutally raped women who fell into their toils.[31]

With the onset of winter, the violence began to subside. The explanation lay in vigorous new measures that put the army back in the field. Frank Angel's investigation had led to the dismissal of Governor Axtell. The new governor, Lew Wallace, obtained a presidential proclamation declaring Lincoln County in a state of insurrection, which again placed the Fort Stanton garrison at the service of civil officers. Wallace then issued his own proclamation—prematurely, as it turned out—announcing the restoration of order.[32]

Wallace's proclamation formed the backdrop for an episode that would gain Billy the Kid national attention and contribute significantly toward his rise into folklore. Hoping to hasten the return of peace, Wallace inserted into his proclamation a measure of dubious wisdom and legality—an amnesty that in effect decriminalized all crimes committed in Lincoln County since the onset of the war. The amnesty cleared away the legal cloud that hung over many of the participants in the war and invited the return of men whom the county could well have done without. But it failed to free Billy Bonney, for it did not apply to offenders already indicted by a grand jury. An indictment stood against the Kid in territorial court for the murder of Sheriff Brady, and another in federal court for the murder of Buckshot Roberts.

On February 18, 1879, exactly one year after Tunstall's death, an incident occurred in Lincoln that positioned Billy Bonney to do something about the murder charges against him. For two months the animosities of the Dolan-McSween feud had been rekindled among the citizens by the almost hysterical agitation of Huston I. Chapman, a noisy and verbose one-armed lawyer imported by Susan McSween to help her wind up the McSween and Tunstall estates. Perhaps not unrelated to the return of partisan passions, some of the leaders in the old fight gathered in Lincoln on February 18 to conclude a formal pact of peace. Among them were Dolan and Mathews, Jesse Evans and one of his particularly vicious desperadoes, Billy Campbell, Bonney, and Tom O'Folliard.

Once their purpose had been concluded, these men and a few others staged a boozy celebration. Staggering down Lincoln's street, they confronted Huston Chapman and began to taunt him. Never one to suffer insult, Chapman replied insolently. Campbell shoved a pistol against the lawyer's chest. Dolan, immediately behind Campbell, drew his pistol and drunkenly fired it into the ground, which prompted Campbell to pull the trigger. Chapman fell to the ground dead, with his clothes set afire by the powder flash.[33]

Although simply a drunken accident, Chapman's murder ignited such a burst of public excitement and fear that Governor Wallace could no longer delay a personal effort to end the travails of Lincoln County. Accompanied by Colonel Edward Hatch, military commander in New Mexico, he set forth from Santa Fe early in March. As a first move, he persuaded Hatch to remove Colonel Dudley from the command of Fort Stanton. Then he turned to others he regarded as prime troublemakers. Many of these, however, enjoyed the immunity granted by Wallace's own amnesty proclamation and thus were beyond his reach. Possibly not beyond reach were Chapman's murderers, including Jesse Evans and Jimmy Dolan himself. As the governor had observed, all he needed were "a few rugged examples."[34]

Wallace also needed a witness who would testify in court and identify the murderers. Bonney swiftly perceived the possibility of a bargain—his testimony in exchange for immunity from the charges against him. On March 13 Billy made the first move, suggesting in a letter to the governor the connection between the Chapman murder and the indictments pending against him. Wallace responded eagerly, and an exchange of messages led to a dramatic secret meeting in Justice Wilson's rude jacal next to the courthouse. And it led finally, on March 21, to the staged "capture" of the Kid and O'Folliard by the new sheriff, George Kimball.[35]

Wallace accorded his prisoner preferred treatment, confining him under guard in a private home rather than in the cellar jail. He also visited him on at least one occasion, when Bonney poured out a long and useful narrative of outlaw personalities and activities.[36] That the patrician governor looked upon his lowly conspirator with condescension, however, may be inferred from a report to Interior Secretary Carl Schurz. "A precious specimen nick-named 'The Kid,'" he wrote, "whom the Sheriff is holding here in the Plaza, . . . is an object of tender regard. I heard singing and music the other night; going to the door, I found the minstrels of the village actually serenading the fellow in his prison."[37] The governor might also have reflected on how much the incident revealed about the stature that his "precious specimen" had already attained in the eyes of many citizens, principally Hispanics.

Wallace had made Billy some sweeping promises. In one of his letters to him, he said that he had authority to exempt him from prosecution, and in the meeting, according to an account many years later, he held up the prospect of a pardon for all past offenses.[38] The Kid kept his part of the bargain, for at the April term of court in Lincoln the grand jury listened to his testimony, and then indicted Campbell and Dolan for murder and Evans and Mathews as accessories. But the governor did not control District Attorney Rynerson, who was as always solicitous of his friend Dolan. "He is bent on going for the Kid," a Wallace associate wrote, and "bent on pushing him to the wall." Rynerson obtained a change of venue to Mesilla, where jurors would be less friendly, and Judge Bristol scheduled the case for later trial.[39]

Bonney's case was but one of an utter chaos of cases that Judge Bristol and his court grappled with in Lincoln during April 1879. The grand jury indicted more than fifty men, some for several offenses. Most pleaded Wallace's amnesty, simply rode out of the county, or ultimately went free because prosecutors declined to prosecute. Although shock waves rolled over the county for years afterward, the April 1879 term of court may be taken as the end of the Lincoln County War.

It also ended William H. Bonney's brief fling at respectability. Whatever the governor's intent, he failed to keep his promise, and Billy needed no one to spell out his probable fate at the hands of Rynerson and Bristol. After testifying at the army court of inquiry that investigated Colonel Dudley's role in the Five-Day Battle, the Kid simply rode out of Lincoln, probably with the full knowledge of Sheriff Kimball. From this point on, he turned to more or less open outlawry. He made several attempts to persuade the governor to help. But Wallace, doubtless rationalizing that the Kid's return to criminal life dissolved any lingering obligation, responded by posting a reward of five hundred dollars for his capture.

Billy the Kid's subsequent adventures as an outlaw chief, and his relentless pursuit by the tireless Sheriff Pat Garrett, form a sequel to the Lincoln County War. Caught, he finally had to face Rynerson and Bristol in trial for Brady's murder. Convicted, he heard the judge pronounce the death sentence. On April 30, 1881, Governor Wallace signed the death warrant.[40] Ironically, two days earlier the Kid had succeeded in his spectacular escape from imprisonment in Lincoln County's newly acquired courthouse—none other than the old Murphy-Dolan store. On a hot July night three months later, Pat Garrett's shots in the dark ended the brief career of Billy the Kid.[41]

The ascent into legend began almost at once, set off by dime novels and the publication of Pat Garrett's *Authentic Life of Billy the Kid*. The legend took on new life and new dimensions in 1926, with the appearance of the enormously influential book by Walter Noble Burns, *The Saga of Billy the Kid*. While pretending to historical accuracy, it contained hardly a hint of fact. A constant stream of books and magazines, fortified by the movies and television, ensured that Billy the Kid, in legend if not in historical truth, would live forever in the world's imagination.

In legend two Billies have struggled for dominance—the psychotic killer, boasting a murder for each of his twenty-one years, and the likable and upright youth marked by great potential for good but driven to crime by the forces of evil. Although neither persona captures reality, suggestions of both may be found in the Billy Bonney of 1877 to 1881.

The killer image springs chiefly from the two-year period following the Lincoln County War, roughly from the summer of 1879 to the summer of 1881. In his twenty-one years, he never came close to twenty-one killings; and during these last two years of his life, only three killings are certain and a fourth possible. But his reputation as an immensely talented outlaw chieftain dates from this time, and the legend draws heavily upon the many postwar adventures. Had the Kid perished with McSween on July 19, 1878, his place in history and folklore would loom no larger than that of Doc Scurlock, Jim French, or John Middleton.

And such, in fact, is the Kid's true significance in the Lincoln County War—the same as that of Scurlock, French, Middleton, and the other Regulators who rode to the banner of Alexander McSween. In like measure was he an outlaw, which is to say that sometimes he stole and even killed. But he and his companions rationalized that they committed such deeds in a sincere attempt to restore a law that had been corrupted by evil men, and the warrants and commissions from the justice of the peace, however legally deficient, gave tangible support to their conviction. Like his fellows, too, the Kid toyed with vague notions of settling down to honest labor. Tunstall's death prevented him from teaming up with Fred Waite to farm on the Peñasco, and he told Governor Wallace that he wanted "to lay aside my arms and go to work." His easy ways and engaging personality contradicted the image of vicious killer and made him a favorite with his friends. Hispanics idolized him.

Thus the Lincoln County War made its contribution to Billy the Kid. For the Kid of legend, it provided a setting for feats of prowess and adventure and acts expressive of character that would be endlessly chronicled with creative hyperbole. For the Kid of history, it provided the influences that shaped his personality from adolescence to manhood. By July 1878, his values closely resembled those of the other Regulators, ambiguously reflecting both the noble and ignoble, and sanctioning a future either for good or for bad. Some of the Regulators turned toward good. The Kid turned the other way.

As for Billy the Kid's contribution to the Lincoln County War, it was the same as that of the other Regulators, no more and no less. Had he never found his way to Lincoln County, the course of the war would almost certainly have remained essentially as history has recorded it.

3
Colonel
Dudley

As Alexander McSween's home burned room by room in the fading light of July 19, 1878, Lieutenant Colonel Nathan A. M. Dudley stayed close to his headquarters tent, located a few hundred yards down Lincoln's only street. Buildings blocked his view, but a thick column of smoke testified to the success of the sheriff's posse in kindling the blaze. Shortly before noon, Dudley and his small command had pitched their tents on a vacant lot near the center of town. He had served notice on both sides in Lincoln's Five-Day Battle that he came to aid neither, and only to protect women and children. If either side endangered his troops, however, he warned that he would blow the offenders into the clouds. At dusk the colonel walked up the street as far as the Tunstall store and looked at the burning McSween home just beyond. But he was in camp when the climax came: flames lighting the night sky, and a sustained rattle of gunfire signaling the escape of Billy the Kid and the death of Alexander McSween.

Dudley's part in the closing scenes of the Five-Day Battle set off a controversy that has echoed ever since in the literature of the Lincoln County War. Did he lead his men from Fort Stanton to Lincoln for humanitarian purposes, as he contended, or to aid the cause of James J. Dolan against lawyer McSween? Did he preserve a strict neutrality, or did he extend active aid, by word or deed, to the Dolan side? Even if scrupulously neutral, did Dudley's mere presence influence the course of the battle or alter its outcome? Despite voluminous evidence, these and other questions still elude conclusive answers.

41

Dudley's own personality fueled the debate. The facade could not have been more militarily imposing—a large, erect frame surmounted by a finely shaped head; a sweeping dragoon mustache, graying hair, and bushy eyebrows shading piercing eyes; a prominent forehead and an assertive nose; and even a monocle suspended from a chain around his neck. Behind the facade, however, lurked a man whose genuine professional dedication consistently fell victim to a small intellect and a huge vanity. He suffered from muddled thought and bad judgment, the result of mediocre endowments impaired by years of dissipation. He got drunk often, and whiskey more or less influenced most of his actions. He compensated for his deficiencies with pomposity, bellicosity, petty despotism, and an extraordinary aptitude for contention. Quick to resent a slight, whether real or imagined, and quick to criticize, whether justly or not, Dudley rocked from one controversy to another throughout his career.

It had not been an outstanding career. Twenty-three years of service had given Dudley the experience to command a frontier fort, but he had been denied the recognition and reward for which he hungered. Seniority had brought him to the rank of lieutenant colonel of the Ninth Cavalry, one of two mounted regiments composed of black troopers and white officers. But his disputatious nature and addiction to the bottle left his trail littered with courts-martial and bitter personal relations with brother officers.[1]

Fresh from a bruising court-martial at Fort Union, Dudley took command of Fort Stanton on April 4, 1878. He arrived ignorant of the issues and personalities that had plunged the area into factional warfare. He knew none of the combatants, headed by Jimmy Dolan on one side, Alex McSween on the other. John H. Tunstall, the ambitious young Englishman who had challenged Dolan's economic domination of Lincoln County, had been killed on February 18, igniting rivalries that had smoldered for a year. On April 1, Billy the Kid and other members of McSween's Regulators had shot down Sheriff William Brady from ambush in Lincoln; and on the very day that Dudley took command, a bloody gunfight rocked Blazer's Mills, near the Mescalero Apache Indian Agency.

Indians, not feuding citizens, were Dudley's main concern. The Mescaleros had a history of unpredictability, occasional thefts, and periodic breakouts. He could muster roughly a hundred men, including black troopers of his own regiment and white footmen of the Fifteenth Infantry. They were too few for their Indian mission, much less for civil duty in addition. But Governor Samuel B. Axtell had urged President Rutherford B. Hayes to provide military aid, and Secretary of War George W. McCrary had instructed the army to assist territorial officials in maintaining order and enforcing legal process in Lincoln County.[2]

These orders had the effect of enlisting the army in one or the other of the two factions battling for supremacy. In aiding Sheriff Brady, Dudley's predecessor had served the Dolan cause, for Brady had ties to Dolan and the warrants he carried were all for McSween and his followers. With Brady's murder, military allegiance shifted, for the new sheriff, John Copeland, turned out to be a McSween tool. He used his army posses to carry out McSween's purposes—until Dudley, incensed, gave him a stern lecture and sent him out to arrest everyone for whom he had warrants, regardless of whether they were McSween or Dolan followers. Then, at the end of May, Dolan maneuvered Copeland out and got the governor to appoint George Peppin, a Dolan tool. Suddenly, the army again rode in the service of Jimmy Dolan.[3]

The Fort Stanton personnel approached their civil mission with mixed feelings. On the one hand, they found the duty itself utterly repugnant. It earned them the ill will of the surrounding community. It wore them out in trying to keep an eye on the Indians while also chasing around the country in usually futile attempts to serve warrants. And it contained the potential for grievous damage to the army as a whole, for the army's heavy-handed part in civil disturbances in the East and the South had brought it under intense political fire. On the other hand, the soldiers felt that the task had to be done. They looked upon themselves as the only effective check on plunder, destruction, and the killing of innocent people.

This belief was soon tested. From motives that had little to do with New Mexico, the U.S. Congress slapped a rider on the army appropriations bill that barred troops from serving as posses for civil officers.[4] The orders reached Colonel Dudley on the night of June 28. He promptly sent couriers to recall a detachment then in the field and served notice that the soldiers could no longer participate in any way in Lincoln County's troubles.[5]

As Dudley foresaw, the abolition of military posses removed the only stabilizing influence from the conflict. It moved swiftly toward a climax. By the middle of July, resolved on a showdown that would settle the issue for good, both the Dolan and McSween forces had taken positions in Lincoln itself. McSween's Regulators numbered close to sixty and divided themselves between the McSween home, the Montaño store, and the Ellis store. Sheriff Peppin had about half as many men, with most of them stationed in the Wortley Hotel, and the rest in the two-story tower, or *torreón*, built years earlier for Indian defense.

Dudley and his officers endured mounting pressures to become involved once again. They cared little for the fate of the two forces, and indeed would have been gratified to see them simply withdraw to the mountains and exterminate each other. But the escalating war took its toll on the innocent, and Dudley had a hard time ignoring their predicament. On July 10 twenty-seven Hispanic women of San Patricio walked twenty miles to Fort Stanton to tell of Peppin's posse tearing up the town and terrorizing the inhabitants. On the thirteenth Sheriff Brady's widow weepingly related how some of McSween's gun-men had tried to kill her eldest son. Two days later Saturnino Baca, a pillar of the Hispanic community, asked Dudley for protection from McSween, who had ordered him out of his home because he allowed Peppin men to occupy the *torreón* next door. "The present status of affairs in the county is simply shameful and disgraceful," Dudley re-ported, and the officers at Fort Stanton all felt mortified that the law prevented them from protecting helpless people.

In fact, so touching were the appeals to his Victorian sensibilities that Dudley began to drift gradually away from the strictly hands-off stance enjoined by his new orders. He sent an officer to investigate the complaints of the San Patricio women. He dispatched his surgeon to attend the wounded of one of the gun battles that led to the occupation of Lincoln. And he stationed a guard at Mrs. Brady's ranch for the protection of her boys. Also, as permitted by his orders, he gave sanctuary at Fort Stanton to anyone who felt threatened by the hostilities.[6]

Dudley also dropped his carefully contrived impartiality. From the first, he had grown increasingly to dislike McSween and his followers. He knew that Peppin's posse contained some of New Mexico's most notorious outlaws, including John Kinney and his gang and Jesse

Evans. But he reasoned that Peppin, denied military posses, had to take whatever fighters he could get or face destruction by McSween's equally bad desperadoes. Also, Peppin, sheriff of Lincoln County by appointment of the governor, operated under a more valid sanction of the law than McSween, who claimed the support only of the justice of the peace and the town constable. On July 16, therefore, in turning down Peppin's request for a howitzer to demolish McSween's house, Dudley spelled out where his sympathies lay and thereby created a record that would haunt him. "Were I not so circumscribed by laws and orders," he declared, "I would most gladly give you every man and material at my post to sustain you in your present position, believing it to be strictly legal."[7]

As the battle for Lincoln grew hotter, two more developments further incensed Dudley. While approaching Lincoln at dusk on July 16, the cavalryman bearing Dudley's reply to Peppin encountered a volley of rifle fire. The bullets tore up the earth and frightened the horse, which reared and threw its rider. The soldier recovered, remounted, and galloped to the safety of the sheriff's headquarters in the Wortley Hotel. Infuriated, Dudley sent a board of officers to Lincoln the next day to conduct an investigation. They not only ascertained that the fire had come from Regulators barricaded in the McSween house, but they found added cause for casting them as villains. A posseman lay wounded within range of the McSween riflemen in the Montaño store. Accompanied by two soldiers, the surgeon and another officer walked out to rescue him and were fired upon from the store. They recovered the wounded man, who died later, and took back to Dudley word of this further insult to the army uniform. They also described the deplorable fate that had befallen the town. The few citizens who had not fled cowered in their homes, unable to go about their business or even venture out for food and water. Women begged the officers to stop the fighting that threatened their lives and those of their children.[8]

Early in the evening of July 18, Dudley summoned the five officers of his command to his quarters. For half an hour they discussed the situation in Lincoln and the danger to women and children, and they quickly decided that humanity demanded some form of military intervention. The orders required by the recent congressional legislation

unequivocally prohibited intervention in civil affairs, but Dudley persuaded himself that a carefully neutral military posture in Lincoln
might serve the purpose without violating the orders. Although mind-
ful of the risks in the decision, all the officers signed a document
recording their concurrence.[9]

Dudley could assemble only a small command. Half his troops were
scouting the Guadalupe and Sacramento mountains for Indians, and
the fort could not be left unguarded. The column that he led to Lincoln
on the morning of July 19 consisted, besides himself, of four officers,
eleven black cavalrymen, and twenty-four white infantrymen. Bringing up the rear, tended by infantry, were a small twelve-pounder
mountain howitzer and a rapid-fire Gatling gun.[10]

The blue column's entry into Lincoln at about 11:00 A.M. inter-
rupted the long-range sniping that had been in progress all morning.
Halting briefly at the Wortley Hotel, Dudley summoned Sheriff Peppin
and declared that the troops had come solely to protect noncombatants, but would return the fire of anyone who fired on them. Near
the center of town, he found an open space slightly east of and across
the street from the Montaño store. Here he decided to camp. His men
pitched tents for the officers and strung a picket line for the cavalry
horses.[11]

Dudley wanted to make certain that no one in Lincoln misun-
derstood his purpose. Twice he sent for Peppin, first to ensure that he
knew where the soldiers were camped, second to repeat his declaration
of neutrality and his warning against any firing that would endanger
the command. He dispatched the same message by written note into
the McSween house, and he summoned Isaac Ellis, whose store contained Regulators, to admonish him in similar language. Finally, he
sent patrols from house to house, and into the surrounding foothills,
to give like notice to everyone and to offer the protection of his camp
to anyone who wanted to come to it.[12]

Even before camping, Dudley momentarily stepped out of his passive role. After learning that the Montaño store harbored about twenty
McSween gunmen, he had the howitzer unlimbered and aimed at the
front door, then sent word that if any bullets came his way he would
blow the house down. The startled defenders, with blankets thrown
over their heads to hide their identity, promptly abandoned the building and hastened down the street to the Ellis store, where they united

with an equal number of comrades.[13] Dudley then swung the howitzer toward the Ellis store, and the entire force evacuated that bastion too. Peppin and some of his posse came running down the street in time to see them on the hills across the Río Bonito to the north. A brief exchange of gunfire marked their withdrawal.[14] When they returned later to the hills behind the McSween house, Dudley had the howitzer and Gatling gun pointed in their direction, and they hastily fell back.[15]

Dudley also availed himself of the occasion to take official notice of the firing on his courier from the McSween house on July 16. He rounded up Justice of the Peace John B. Wilson, a prominent McSween supporter, and instructed him to issue a warrant for McSween's arrest on charges of attempting to kill the soldier. When Wilson resisted, Dudley threatened to place him in double irons and report him to the governor for failing in his duty. Easily intimidated, the old man did as he was told.[16]

Dudley also had an acrimonious conversation with Susan Mc-Sween, who came to his camp to appeal for her husband's life. No novice herself at invective, Susan gave as good as she received. But Dudley loftily maintained that he could not interfere with the sheriff in the discharge of his duty. McSween harbored known outlaws, he pointed out, and was resisting a legally constituted posse armed with legally issued warrants for their arrest. They could stop the battle at any time simply by giving up to the law. Susan begged Dudley to allow her husband to surrender to him rather than to Peppin. Dudley refused.[17]

All afternoon, therefore, the posse pressed the attack unhampered by soldiers. Near dusk, Dudley sent a party to help in moving the possessions of a family temporarily living in the Tunstall store. Three Regulators posted there were sniping at the men besieging the McSween house next door, and a deputy made ready to burn them out too. Strolling up the street to the store at this time, Dudley passed a few words with Peppin, who was loosely directing the fight from the top floor of the *torreón*, and told him that if his men persisted in the destruction of property he would have to interfere.[18] Shortly afterward, the McSween fighters fled both the store and the house, and the store escaped the torch. In this final burst of firing, McSween died and the Five-Day Battle ended.

Next morning, accompanied by his surgeon, Dudley again walked up the street to the Tunstall store. Drawn by a loud commotion inside, they entered. Peppin and many of his posse crowded the store. Dry goods and other merchandise littered the counters and the floor. Outlaw John Kinney was there. So was outlaw Jesse Evans, stripped to his underwear and trying on a new suit. The officers watched the chaotic scene for about five minutes, then returned to camp. That afternoon, Dudley struck camp and led the command back to Fort Stanton.[19]

On the battlefield of Lincoln, now silent and smoking, Colonel Dudley left the makings of a controversy that burst over him and the army. Inflamed by his own abrasive and quarrelsome disposition, the dispute centered on whether, actively or passively, he had decided the outcome of the fight between Dolan and McSween. Almost a year later an army court cleared him. History has not been so generous. But neither has history been either definitive or persuasive.

The case against Dudley began with his motives for going to Lincoln at all. His enemies charged that he had rushed in with the fixed purpose of helping Peppin, and indeed in response to a plea from Dolan on July 18 to come to his aid. Dudley argued that he had gone solely to protect women and children. All of his officers backed him in the explanation. Neither he nor his officers had any personal stake in the outcome of the struggle. They leaned toward Dolan and Peppin simply because they represented more substantial institutions of law than McSween. But for a week evidence had piled up of the grave danger in which the battle had placed defenseless citizens, and the officers agonized over the plight of helpless women and children. Moreover, they foresaw the public outrage that would fall on the army if any women or children were killed while the troops remained aloof at Fort Stanton. Dudley may have thought that he could have it both ways, that he could protect noncombatants without interfering in civil affairs. More likely, he had looked to a big show of neutrality to provide a defense against official reproach. Without much question, Dudley went to Lincoln chiefly for the reason that he said he went, and he could not properly have resolved his dilemma in any other way.[20]

Dudley's entry into Lincoln decisively altered the balance of power. The McSween people outnumbered their attackers and could not have been dislodged from their positions without unacceptable casualties. The appearance of troops, coupled with the notice that they would return the fire of anyone whose bullets came their way, gave the attackers a crucial advantage: they could attack, but the defenders could not shoot back without the risk of hitting a soldier.

Unable to contain his natural bluster, and probably stimulated by an occasional nip at the bottle,[21] Dudley went a step beyond a mere passive presence and pointed his artillery menacingly at the Montaño and Ellis stores. This forced the evacuation of Lincoln by two-thirds of McSween's men. They played no further part in the battle. Thus Peppin, heretofore badly outnumbered, now found himself with two-to-one odds and with the enemy positions reduced from four to two. Dudley justified his handling of the artillery as elementary precautions for self-defense in case of attack, a technicality that scarcely diluted his responsibility for the decisive event of the battle.

In view of this action, the McSween forces could hardly be blamed for believing that the soldiers had come to help Peppin, a belief that later expanded to include their active participation. Occupants of the McSween house and Tunstall store recalled soldiers standing about and even helping to fuel the blaze, and Billy the Kid and a companion in the final escape told of three soldiers firing on them from the southwest corner of the Tunstall store. In fact, Dudley gave strict orders that no soldiers could leave camp unless authorized. They had no reason to disobey, certainly not to risk their lives in a fight that did not even remotely concern them. Enough soldiers left on routine assignments from Dudley, however, to constitute a conspicuous military presence in Lincoln and to give rise to the conviction of the McSween people that the army supported the enemy. Adding to the impression, several possemen wore old military jackets or trousers.[22]

Dudley needlessly invited criticism by bullying Justice of the Peace Wilson. The warrant for McSween's arrest that Dudley forced Wilson to issue had no effect on the events of the day. Peppin already had warrants for McSween and virtually all of the Regulators. He did not need another to claim legal sanction for his attack on the McSween forces. Dudley's enemies made much of this episode, as if he sought the warrant to justify his presence, but its principal significance was to betray the colonel's sympathies and convict him of bad timing and bad judgment. He need not have chosen this particular day to make an issue of the matter.

Dudley's bombast toward Susan McSween further damaged his

credibility and gained him an enemy of formidable powers. She also confronted him with a dilemma to which he proved entirely insensitive. He had come to town to protect women and children. The McSween house contained two women and five children. He might have seized on this pretext to accept McSween's surrender, as Susan pleaded. He was technically correct, of course, in declining to interfere with the sheriff. But he had already intervened in civil matters simply by marching into Lincoln, and the added risk could not have been so great if explained by the wish to end bloodshed. He surely knew that if McSween surrendered to the sheriff, he would be killed on one pretext or another before he could ever come to trial. As further rationale, as McSween himself pointed out in a note to Dudley, the precinct constable, one of the Regulators, had legal warrants from the justice of the peace for the arrest of Peppin and most of his posse. What better course than to stop the fighting and let the courts decide? Instead, he climbed on his high plane of noninterference, leaving Susan and the other woman and the children to seek safety elsewhere and McSween and three others to perish in the final shootout.

In addition to all of the other accusations, Dudley discovered himself charged with abetting and even participating in the looting of the Tunstall store on July 20. In truth, he briefly watched Peppin's men ransack the store without protesting. But unless Jesse Evans walked out in a new suit, which is uncertain, the store was not looted before the troops returned to their station in the afternoon. The plunder of the contents occurred that night and the next day, and some of the noncombatants whom Dudley had come to protect shared the adventure with the jubilant posse.[23]

Although the military court of inquiry that probed Dudley's conduct swept away all of the allegations and even bestowed generous compliments, the evidence presented to the court gives him a different place in history than in military law. Quite simply, had the troops remained at Fort Stanton, McSween would not have lost the battle. They came, and McSween lost—everything. Dudley was the critical factor in that result.

Dudley went to Lincoln for the right reasons, even though prohibited by orders. Once there, by his words he showed his partiality for Peppin, and by his deeds he gave decisive assistance to Peppin. However technically persuasive to a military court, the rationale for these words and deeds rings hollow in history. Yet, ironically, even the most passive role could not have avoided influencing the battle in favor of Peppin. Only by abandoning all pretense of noninterference and simply stopping the fight could Dudley have brought about a different result. In retrospect, this is what he should have done.

A master at self-justification, Dudley easily convinced himself of the rectitude of his every action in Lincoln. That instead they traced a bewilderingly erratic course escaped him entirely. He deeply, and correctly, believed that he went to town for unimpeachable reasons. His grand show of neutrality convinced almost no one of his neutrality, but it truly convinced him. Neutrality justified his refusal to save McSween and to interfere with the impending looting of the Tunstall store. A military technicality rationalized a departure from neutrality in the handling of his artillery, a legal technicality the browbeating of Justice Wilson, a sudden impulse to avoid further destruction his warning against burning the Tunstall store. In Dudley's mind, all fell logically and defensibly into place, and he genuinely believed that he had behaved responsibly and humanely.

Ironically, although reported in detail to his superiors, Dudley's foray into Lincoln on July 19 and 20 earned him no reprimand—indeed, no official notice at all. In the absence of any public protest, the army chain of command was not about to give prominence to a politically sensitive issue. Dudley would probably have escaped official scrutiny altogether except for a further embroilment with Susan McSween and, through her, with the new governor of New Mexico, Lew Wallace.

The distraught widow held Dudley chiefly responsible for the death of her husband, and in Las Vegas she found an ally to help press her case. Recently arrived from Oregon, Huston I. Chapman was a excitable and verbose young lawyer with one arm and a talent for hyperbole fully the equal of Dudley's. Susan engaged him to help her in settling the McSween estate, but Chapman quickly took up her cause against Dudley. In a letter of October 24, 1878, he informed Governor Wallace that he could prove Dudley "criminally responsible" for McSween's death. Moreover, Mrs. McSween had fled Lincoln because of fear of Dudley, and now she was afraid to return even though her affairs there needed attention.[24]

Wallace thought Chapman's accusations "incredible." They were also disquieting, for the governor's plans for ending the troubles in Lincoln County depended heavily upon Colonel Dudley. At Wallace's instigation, President Hayes had proclaimed Lincoln County in a state of insurrection and had commanded all dissidents to disband and return to their homes by October 13. After that date, the army could lawfully take up the civil duties prohibited by Congress the previous June. As the commander on the scene, Dudley would be the key figure. Wallace, therefore, sent Chapman's letter to the commander of the military district, Colonel Edward Hatch, who forwarded it on to Dudley for comment.[25]

Dudley reacted with typical bombast. Disdaining even to comment, he enclosed eight affidavits that attacked Susan McSween as ruthless, dishonest, and scandalously immoral but that dealt only briefly and superficially with the events of July 20. Although clearly unresponsive, Wallace pronounced the reply "perfectly satisfactory," and then unwittingly proceeded to antagonize Dudley further.[26]

For a month, Dudley's weekly reports had told of no serious breach of the peace in Lincoln County. Anxious to believe the troubles already ended, Wallace drafted a proclamation declaring them ended. Hoping to hasten the return to tranquillity, he included a passage granting amnesty to everyone charged with crime who had not been actually indicted by a grand jury. Before the proclamation's release, however, Chapman visited Wallace in Santa Fe and announced that, at the next term of district court, he and McSween's friends intended to begin criminal proceedings against Dudley for murder and arson. Thinking to provide a defense against such harassment, Wallace pulled out his draft proclamation and inserted a phrase extending the amnesty to all army officers.[27]

Issued on November 13, 1878, Wallace's proclamation stunned Dudley, who reacted with typically mindless spontaneity. Though not ignorant of the governor's motivation, he chose to interpret the intended favor as a slander on him and his officers. He struck back in a rambling "open letter" that rejected the extension of the amnesty to the military and blasted Wallace for the implication of criminal guilt that he believed it threw over the Fort Stanton officers. Published in the Santa Fe *New Mexican* on December 14, the polemic was both a grave official impropriety and a personal insult to the governor of the territory.[28]

Even before publication of the open letter, Wallace had decided that Dudley had to go. Huston Chapman had written him two long and emotional letters from Lincoln. Though full of partisan excess, they clearly showed that Dudley had aroused enough local antagonisms to unfit him for his post. The time had therefore come, the governor advised Colonel Hatch on December 7, to send to Fort Stanton an officer with no prior involvement in the hostilities or connections to the principal personalities. Hatch backed away from so delicate an issue, as did his superiors all the way to the top. But General-in-Chief William Tecumseh Sherman met it head-on. He refused to injure Dudley's reputation by relieving him for no other reason than the request of a civil official, and Secretary of War McCrary backed him. A vindicated Dudley filed the papers for future reference and chalked up another grievance against the governor.[29]

Dudley quickly found other grievances. Aside from the insult to army officers, Wallace's proclamation of November 13 created serious problems for Dudley and his command. He had just received orders to aid in putting down the insurrection proclaimed by President Hayes. Yet here was Wallace with his own proclamation declaring peace and order restored in Lincoln County. Did that mean the army should no longer support civil authorities? Lawyer Chapman thought so, and he did little to promote peace by counseling Lincoln residents to shoot any army officer who tried to arrest them. Wallace attempted to clear up the confusion by stating that the peace and order he had proclaimed depended on continued military intervention, but that explanation failed to put the issue to rest.[30]

Dudley scoffed at the notion that the troubles had ended. After a lull, they had resumed with fresh intensity, in part because of the governor's proclamation. Promised amnesty, many who had fled the county now came back. Moreover, sheriffs and army officers hesitated to make arrests, "not knowing who is pardoned and who is not." "If His Excellency Governor Wallace thinks peace and order prevails in Lincoln County," Dudley wrote in mid-December, "he is the worst fooled official I ever saw."[31]

In addition to rampant rustling and general lawlessness throughout the county, the old Dolan-McSween rivalries broke out anew. In Lincoln, Chapman and Susan kept up a shrill agitation, and the return

of prominent Regulators like Doc Scurlock and Billy Bonney heightened the danger of new violence. Dudley made matters worse by
placing Fort Stanton off limits to such "murderers and rustlers," whom
he identified by name even though not convicted of any crime, and
among whom he included Huston Chapman.[32]

Dudley also incurred abuse as a result of the misbehavior of one
of his officers, an immature youth with a large thirst for whiskey.
Commanding a military posse under Sheriff Peppin, Lieutenant James
H. French grievously overstepped his authority by forcing his way into
Susan's home, engaging in a profane shouting match with Chapman,
and stripping to the waist to settle matters with one arm tied behind
his back—a manly deference to Chapman's infirmity. Chapman brought
charges against French in Justice Wilson's court, but a board of officers
exonerated him in military eyes, and Dudley sent him to an assignment
safely distant from the county seat.[33]

Susan's attorney had not only succeeded her husband as a leading
feudist, but he brought to the role a hysteria that made him more
dangerous. "Chapman," reported Dudley, "is credited with doing more
at the present time to keep the community in a state of excitement
than any other man in the county, not excepting Jim French, Kidd,
or any of that clique."[34]

Others felt the same way, so much so that some of the leaders of
both sides, including Jimmy Dolan and Billy Bonney, took the extraordinary step of arranging a peace conference to try to prevent the
war from breaking out again. On the night of February 18, 1879, a
dozen or more assembled in Lincoln and worked out the terms of an
agreement. Then, in the course of a drunken celebration, they met
Chapman on the street, got into an altercation, and shot and killed
him. The man who pulled the trigger was William Campbell, a hard
case from the Pecos who worked for Dolan.[35]

Already apprehensive over the gathering of so many veterans of
past hostilities, Lincoln's residents now shuddered in fear that Chapman's murder would set off another battle between McSween and
Dolan gunmen. Citizens united to plead with Dudley for military
protection, and the new sheriff, George Kimball, obliged with the
necessary documentation. Dudley sent troops, and he himself went to
town for the first time since July 19. He found himself greeted as the
savior of Lincoln. People who only recently had vied with one another

in excoriating the colonel made a public meeting ring with expressions of gratitude and respect.[36]

Dudley's name evoked no such fine sentiments in the executive chambers in Santa Fe. To all the other demerits against Dudley, Wallace now added the suspicion of complicity in the slaying of Chapman. The suggestion came from Ira E. Leonard, an asthmatic associate of Chapman who was equally meddlesome but not so hyperactive. Only a few days before his murder, Chapman had confided to Leonard his fear that Colonel Dudley and Lieutenant French were plotting his death, and Leonard knew of other circumstances, he informed Wallace, that in retrospect added up to "proof as strong as holy writ."[37] As confirmation of sorts, several witnesses overheard Campbell declare, immediately after the shooting, that "he had promised his God and General Dudley that he would kill Chapman, and he had done it."[38]

The Chapman murder prompted Wallace finally to visit Lincoln. He arrived on March 5, having traveled with Colonel Hatch. High on his agenda was the removal of Colonel Dudley. He had already persuaded Hatch of the necessity. All that remained was a formal request, which he took up to Fort Stanton on March 8. In order to bring criminals to justice, he wrote, he had to have witnesses to swear affidavits as the basis for legal proceedings, and these he could not obtain because people feared retaliation through Dudley's misuse of military power. They held him responsible for McSween's death and also believed him to be implicated in Chapman's murder. Wallace did not know the truth of these allegations, he said, but he had become convinced that the fears of the citizens were not irrational. Hatch promptly issued orders relieving Dudley of his command and posting him to Fort Union to await action by higher authority. Jubilant, Wallace returned to Lincoln on the evening of March 8 and called a public meeting to boast that he had accomplished "the best day's work ever done for the citizens of Lincoln County."[39]

Colonel Dudley erupted in almost incoherent rage. He had been unjustly relieved and his reputation smeared without any chance to offer a defense or even know what the specific accusations were or who had made them. The records of the fort and twenty witnesses within a ten-mile radius could "annihilate totally" every charge against him. Yet neither Wallace nor Hatch would take time to talk with him, even though they passed the afternoon of March 8 at "a convivial dinner given at the post." The Secretary of War himself had ruled that Dudley should not be relieved on petition of the governor. Even so, he telegraphed the Adjutant General of the army, "I am disgraced without a hearing and deprived of even preparing a defense." In a follow-up letter, and in a long personal letter to General Sherman, Dudley poured out his indignation and demanded a court of inquiry.[40]

Unknown to either Dudley or Wallace, legal proceedings had already been launched. On March 4 Ira Leonard, the Las Vegas lawyer, had mailed what he labeled "charges and specifications" to the Secretary of War. Among other offenses, Dudley stood accused of aiding in the murder of McSween, the burning of his house, and the looting of the Tunstall store as well as of vague evils growing out of the open letter to Wallace, the slander of Susan McSween, and the misconduct of Lieutenant French in Lincoln. Significantly, while enclosing a newspaper account that connected Dudley with the murder of Chapman, Leonard did not include this offense among his charges. Apparently, on reflection, he decided that his "proof as strong as holy writ" might not stand up in court. Although not in proper military form and failing even elementary requirements of legal precision, Leonard's "charges and specifications" became the basis for the court of inquiry ordered in response to Dudley's request.[41]

Ira Leonard not only prepared the charges, he prosecuted them. When the court finally went to work at Fort Stanton on May 9, 1879, he appeared in person as assistant to the "recorder," the equivalent in a court of inquiry of the prosecutor, and actually did most of the examination and cross-examination in presenting the case against Dudley. He explained his motives as simply high-minded public service. In fact, he not only had succeeded Chapman as Susan McSween's attorney but had come down to Lincoln to labor in behalf of Governor Wallace. During the April term of district court he had acted as a special prosecutor by appointment of the governor, who trusted neither the district judge nor the prosecuting attorney.[42] So faithfully had he carried out this mission that he stayed to perform a similar role in the Dudley court. His zeal for the public benefit may have been encouraged by an explicit understanding that Wallace would try to get President Hayes to dismiss Judge Warren Bristol and replace him with Ira Leonard.[43]

During the first sessions of the court, Leonard thought he had Dudley on the run. "I tell you," he wrote the governor on May 23, "we are pouring the 'hot shot' into Dudley so fiercely that his face for the last three days has strikingly resembled the wattles of an enraged turkey gobbler." But the euphoria soon turned to gloom. Ruling after ruling of the court thwarted Leonard or favored Dudley. This was due less to the court's resolve to whitewash Dudley than to the adroitness of Dudley's defense counsel. In Henry L. Waldo, Attorney General of New Mexico, Leonard more than met his match. Waldo was an able and respected lawyer with an eloquence exceeded only by his devastating sarcasm. Between Waldo's courtroom skill and the court's desire to protect one of its own, Dudley emerged victorious. The court concluded that none of the allegations had been proved and therefore that proceedings before a court-martial were unnecessary.[44]

Higher authority took a long time to review the record. Not until December 1879 did the military bureaucracy come forth with a final disposition of the case, and then only after nudged by Dudley. The delay hid a disagreement within the army. Hatch's superior, General John Pope, took issue with the court's findings and drew up papers to bring Dudley before a court-martial. In Washington, however, the Judge Advocate General of the army pronounced the court's findings convincing and predicted that an expensive court-martial would reach the same conclusion. Doubtless with some relief, the Secretary of War decided against Pope. On December 30, General Sherman directed that all proceedings against Dudley cease and that he be given a new command.[45]

In addition to the court of inquiry, Dudley fought other legal battles in 1879. Represented by Ira Leonard, Susan McSween sued for twenty-five thousand dollars in libel, alleging defamation of character in the affidavits of November 1879; but she failed to press the suit to legal conclusion. More seriously, at the April term of district court in Lincoln, the grand jury indicted Dudley, together with former sheriff Peppin and outlaw John Kinney, for arson in the burning of the McSween home. Pleading the impossibility of a fair trial in Lincoln, Dudley won a change of venue to Doña Ana County, and he persuaded Judge Bristol to order Susan McSween to appear as a witness. Dudley also convinced the U.S. Attorney General that the charges grew out of the performance of his official duties and that he therefore should be defended by the United States attorney for New Mexico. When Dudley finally came to trial in Mesilla late in November, Susan failed to appear. She sent word that her attorney, Ira Leonard, had not called for her, and she asked for postponement to a later term of court. Judge Bristol angrily refused, and she belatedly showed up. After three days of heated legal contention, the jury returned a verdict of not guilty, and the spectators broke into cheers and applause.[46]

Dudley expected to return to Fort Stanton to savor his triumph, but Hatch assigned him to Fort Union instead. Hatch also tried to rid the army of him altogether, alleging unfitness for any duty wrought by decades of dissipation, but Dudley's vindication by both military and civil courts persuaded the army hierarchy to leave well enough alone. Years later, when Dudley accidentally learned of Hatch's attempt, he smugly called attention to his record in the campaign against the Apache Victorio in 1880. Commanding the cavalry component of an expedition that marched a punishing seven hundred miles across the Mexican deserts, he claimed to have been the senior officer and yet the only officer who had never once taken refuge in a wagon or ambulance. Seniority made Dudley a full colonel in 1885 and brought him to retirement in 1889—coincidentally, almost exactly four months after his old antagonist, Edward Hatch, had died from injuries sustained in a carriage accident. Dudley lived out a quiet retirement in Roxbury, Massachusetts, and died in 1910, with his last six years sweetened by promotion to brigadier general on the retired list.[47]

In an autobiographical sketch written for his military record at about the time of his retirement, Colonel Dudley depicted himself as a major figure in the Lincoln County War. He sketched a self-portrait of the principled humanitarian determined to surmount towering obstacles in order to save the women and children of Lincoln. In this worthy purpose he succeeded, only to be persecuted by "McSween's renegades" for the very crimes that they themselves had committed. Although this was an egotistical self-deception typical of Dudley's entire life, he truthfully remembered his part as significant. Indeed, it was decisive. He could not have won the war for McSween. He assuredly lost the war for McSween.[48]

Colonel Dudley was not a likable fellow. But neither were any of the other principals in the Lincoln County War. At least he was basically sincere, as few of them were. He wanted to do his military duty as law, justice, and humanity demanded. Personal limitations made that ideal impossible to achieve. In particular, whiskey muddied his thinking and impaired his judgment. So bitter an enemy as Colonel Hatch thought whiskey to be the key ingredient in Dudley's performance. "If Dudley had not been so constantly under the influence of liquor while at Stanton," Hatch wrote confidentially to Governor Wallace, "he might have managed matters very well. I attach the most of his trouble to drink."[49] It was true throughout his life, and it goes far to explain his erratic conduct in the Lincoln County War.

4
Lew
Wallace

As the bullets of the Dolan-Peppin posse riddled Alexander McSween in the backyard of his burning home in Lincoln on the night of July 19, 1878, Lew Wallace suffered a restless boredom in his hometown of Crawfordsville, Indiana. His law practice afforded none of the adventure and romance that he craved and that he had occasionally sampled in a varied political and military career spanning three decades. He found vicarious compensation in literary pastimes. One novel had proved moderately successful, and now he labored on another, a sweeping saga of biblical times whose hero he named Ben-Hur.

Wallace anxiously awaited a presidential summons to more exciting pursuits. His services to the Republican Party in the disputed presidential election of 1876 had put the Hayes administration greatly in his debt, and for more than a year he had impatiently anticipated his reward. Appointment as minister to Bolivia held no appeal, and he turned down the invitation. The territorial governorship of New Mexico probably seemed no better. But perhaps fearing no further offers, when sounded out for the post in August 1878 he said that he would accept.[1]

The actual appointment hung on the fate of the incumbent governor, Samuel B. Axtell. Austere, vain, and both impulsive and inflexible in his judgments, Axtell had been a conscientious governor, probably the best New Mexico had been given since falling to the United States by conquest in the Mexican War. But Axtell was also uncritical of designing friends and too easily influenced by them. He had been led into some unwise decisions in the imbroglio of Lincoln County, and, not altogether justly, he confronted the humiliation of dismissal.

Sentiment for Axtell's suspension had been building in Washington since the previous spring. Several partisans of Alexander McSween with ties to the Hayes administration had written influential letters assailing Axtell's course in the war between the rival commercial empires of James J. Dolan and the slain Englishman, John H. Tunstall. But the most insistent demand for meaningful action came from the British minister in Washington, who was understandably perturbed over the slaying of one of Her Majesty's subjects. In April 1878, his pressures on the State Department led to the appointment of a young New York lawyer and Republican patronage seeker, Frank Warner Angel, as a government agent charged with investigating the mess in New Mexico. Angel did not submit his written report until October 1878, but an August meeting in Washington with Secretary of the Interior Carl Schurz, the official to whom territorial governors reported, doomed Axtell.[2]

The New Mexico vacancy presented an opportunity to try once more to satisfy the patronage claims of Lew Wallace. On August 31 Schurz advised President Hayes that the oral report of Angel had convinced him of the need for a change in Santa Fe, and "the sooner the better." As Wallace had said he would serve, "we ought to have him on the spot as speedily as possible." On September 4 the word went forth to Crawfordsville. Rescued at last, Wallace hastened to Washington for a briefing by Angel, then faced west. On the night of September 30, stiff, sore, and utterly exhausted, he "crawled off" the buckboard that had brought him from the railhead in Colorado and took refuge in La Fonda, the inn on the Santa Fe plaza across from the governor's "palace."[3]

New Mexico had gained no ordinary party hack such as presidents usually sent to this remote territory as a reward for political services. At fifty-one, Lew Wallace looked back on a career of genuine distinction, one that testified to uncommon merit. A youthful tour with Indiana volunteers in the Mexican War had kindled a martial ardor that flamed ever more brightly with advancing age. Militia service led to high rank in the Union army early in the Civil War. But at Shiloh General Wallace took longer to get his division to the battlefield than General Ulysses S. Grant thought warranted, and his chances for military fame and glory fell victim to Grant's need for a scapegoat. Before returning to civil life at the war's end, Wallace served in other posts, including a military commission that tried the assassins of Abraham Lincoln and another that condemned the Confederate commander of the Andersonville prison camp. But he never regained the prestige and authority that he had enjoyed before Shiloh, and the resulting sense of injustice proved to be a lifelong obsession. His quest for vindication, sometimes tactless and self-defeating, irritated General and later President Grant as well as General William T. Sherman, Grant's friend and also a Shiloh commander. In 1878 Sherman headed the army, and Governor Wallace could have profited from his friendly cooperation.

Wallace looked and acted like a governor. A thick, short beard and bushy mustache covered much of his face, while his hair fell carelessly across a high forehead. Eyeglasses perched on the bridge of his nose. "Tall and slender," wrote a newsman who interviewed him on the eve of his departure for New Mexico, with "the weather-beaten face and military bearing indicative of the trained soldier, a piercing black eye, and decision of character written in every lineament of his countenance. An active life in the field has left its traces on his face and sprinkled his raven hair with gray. His manner is frank and courteous and his conversational power great."[4] Lawyer, politician, soldier, scholar, philosopher, musician, artist, author, sportsman, restless adventurer, and ambitious public figure, Lew Wallace brought to his post a sharpness of intellect, a range of abilities, and a breadth of interests unrivaled by any predecessor.

Governor Wallace at once plunged into his new duties. He had been sent to New Mexico to clean up Lincoln County, and within five days of taking the oath of office he had gathered evidence to support bold measures. From Colonel Edward Hatch, commander of the military district, he obtained the dispatches of Lieutenant Colonel Nathan A. M. Dudley at Fort Stanton. Immobilized by a recent act of Congress that barred the army from aiding civil authorities, Dudley could only look on in helpless fury as bands of murderous outlaws roamed Lincoln County robbing, killing, raping, and plundering. Judge Warren Bristol reported that the fall term of district court could not be held in safety, and anyway the citizens were too terrorized to function as witnesses or jurors. U.S. Marshal John Sherman declared himself powerless to serve federal arrest warrants.

Citing these opinions, on October 5 Wallace telegraphed his rec-
ommendations to Secretary Schurz. With the army, the sheriff, the
marshal, and the courts impotent and the territory without a militia,
he said, only one recourse remained: martial law. He urged Schurz to
see the President and seek a proclamation placing Lincoln County
under martial law, suspending the writ of habeas corpus, and establishing a military commission to try all offenders.[5]

The Hayes administration reacted swiftly but met Wallace only
halfway. To use troops to apprehend criminals seemed defensible; to
use them to try, convict, and sentence criminals was not politically
palatable. In a fence-straddling proclamation of October 7, therefore,
President Hayes declared Lincoln County in a state of insurrection
and commanded all dissidents to disband and return to their homes
by October 13. After that date, the army could lawfully furnish posses
again to civil authorities.[6]

This was hardly the martial law for which Wallace had asked, and
he thought the measure badly flawed. "To refer the matter to the civil
authorities is childish," he wired Schurz with a fine disregard for official
protocol. Lincoln County suffered as much from a paralyzed court as
a paralyzed sheriff; for troops to help in catching criminals served no
purpose if the courts could not try and punish them. The judiciary
could not be expected to function, he declared, "when courts must
sit surrounded by bayonets, and juries deliberate in dread of assassination." The only solution was "to make war upon the murderous
bands," and that meant martial law.[7]

But Wallace made the best of what he had been given. No one
seemed quite sure of the next move. On October 26, therefore, Wallace finally took it upon himself to lay before Colonel Hatch a proposed
program for employing the army to pacify the war zone. Hatch oblig-
ingly framed instructions for Colonel Dudley that reflected Wallace's
thinking as well as his own orders from Washington to disperse "un-
lawful combinations" that had failed to heed the President's command.
Dispatched the very next day, October 27, Hatch's orders required
Dudley to provide the sheriff with military posses upon request but
also, even in the absence of requests, to take the initiative in rounding
up and confining criminals.[8]

Even before these orders went out, Wallace had persuaded himself
that the President's proclamation was working. Little more than a
week after he had branded it "childish," he informed Schurz that it

had produced a "sufficient effect" and that he hoped martial law could be avoided.[9] Except for generally favorable press coverage, Wallace had no evidence on which to base his new assessment, but he had suddenly acquired good reason for wishing it so. Rumors flew that political enemies sought to head off his confirmation in the U.S. Senate, and he wanted to be able to say that he had already done what he had been sent to New Mexico to do.

Although Schurz thought Wallace's alarm unfounded, worry over his confirmation probably motivated the governor's next move. Needing a show of success to offset the opposition, Wallace simply declared success. Two dispatches from Colonel Dudley reported no recent crime or violence, so on November 13 Wallace issued his own proclamation announcing the end of disorders in Lincoln County and inviting residents to resume their normal occupations. To foster the return to peace and normalcy, Wallace extended a "general pardon" to all offenders not already indicted by a grand jury.[10]

The governor's proclamation met with the disapproval of New Mexico's newspapers. "Of course the Governor is desirous of being confirmed," editorialized the *Mesilla Independent*, "and the most peaceful aspect of affairs will be the more conducive to that result." In fact, a lull in "the murdering of people in cold blood" had occurred, conceded the *Mesilla News*, but peace had not returned, and "the people are living in daily expectation and fear of a recurrence of lawlessness." Only the sight of bluecoats on the roads and in the settlements restrained new outbreaks of violence. Reports from Colonel Dudley throughout late November and early December fully sustained the opinions of the press.

The amnesty attracted even more criticism. The *New Mexican* thought it "granted undeserved grace" to malefactors, the *News* branded it "outrageous," and the *Independent* pronounced it both illegal and improper. "The bad element," according to the *Independent*, "along with the good are invited to return and still apply their nefarious vocations." Again, Dudley's dispatches substantiated the charge. Men who had fled the county rather than face military arrest now returned, secure in the protection of the governor's pardon.[11]

In another way the amnesty brought grief upon Wallace, for with it he unthinkingly made a bitter enemy of Colonel Dudley. At the last moment, he had inserted language including army officers within the provisions of the amnesty. He had done this simply to protect

Dudley from legal harassment. Aided by a mercurial Las Vegas lawyer, Huston I. Chapman, Alexander McSween's widow laid plans to charge Dudley in civil court with the murder of her husband and the burning of her home in the final battle for Lincoln the previous July. In the pardon, therefore, Wallace thought to give Dudley a legal defense that would spare him the trouble and expense of a court battle. But Dudley, a vain and temperamental controversialist, bristled over the imputation that he or his officers had been guilty of any wrongdoing, much less criminal offense. In a burst of outrage, he wrote a long, insulting, and barely coherent open letter to the governor and had it published in the Santa Fe *New Mexican*.[12]

Dudley's public attack on Wallace intensified a mutual disenchantment that, although they had never met, had been growing for more than a month. Late in October, Huston Chapman gave Wallace a lurid account of Dudley's role in the July battle for Lincoln. Asked to comment, Dudley overreacted with a sheaf of affidavits assailing the character and chastity of Chapman's client, Susan McSween. Wallace tried to soothe Dudley's indignation, but further sensational reports from Chapman convinced the governor that, however unintentionally, Dudley had become so entangled in the local feuding as to destroy his usefulness. Even before publication of the open letter, therefore, Wallace asked Hatch to send another officer to Fort Stanton. Bursting into print a week later, the open letter only confirmed Wallace in his judgment, and also, in muddying the confirmation issue, it probably stirred in Wallace thoughts of revenge.[13]

Wallace's request for Dudley's relief sent shock waves up the army chain of command. Privately, Colonel Hatch was receptive; he and Wallace got along well, while he and Dudley had been bitter enemies for almost a decade. But Wallace had alleged no misconduct, only that Dudley had excited local animosities. Hatch therefore forwarded the request to higher headquarters, and so it made its way to the very top. There, General Sherman rebelled against such civilian meddling in military affairs, and he rejected the application with an indignation perhaps heightened by resentment over the applicant's stubborn agitation of old Shiloh disputes.[14] In due course, the papers made their way to Dudley, who filed them in elated satisfaction.

Not only for his proclamation did Wallace provoke criticism. "As to Lincoln County," he had wired Schurz on the very day he took office, "I shall go see the people immediately." Yet he had not gone.

Huston Chapman scolded him in intemperate language and warned of dire consequences. Dudley delightedly called attention to the governor's failure to investigate in person. The newspapers took up the cry. Late in December Wallace lamely explained that he could have gone to neither town nor fort without arousing bad feeling at the other, "so I stayed away from both, and am well satisfied that I did so."[15]

In truth, Wallace either convinced himself of the accuracy of his proclamation or simply lost interest in Lincoln County, or both. The explanation probably sprang in large part from a competing preoccupation. He had resumed work on his novel. Each night he withdrew to an inner room of the ancient Palace of the Governors and, in the glow of a "student's-lamp," spun more adventures for the fictional Ben-Hur. Nudged by the vicarious immediacy of the Holy Land, Lincoln County receded to the far corners of his mind.[16]

Meanwhile, in Lincoln County, events tended to support Wallace's first evaluation of the President's proclamation. The sheriff and his deputies could call on troops to help in arresting criminals, but the absence of effective judicial machinery made the effort a futile labor. Judge Warren Bristol would not hold district court in Lincoln until April, if then. In the meantime, Justice of the Peace John B. Wilson presided over the only court in which offenders could be arraigned and bound over for trial. He was an ignorant and confused old man whose rulings defied law and logic and whose sympathies lay with the McSween faction. Colonel Dudley fumed in frustration over Wilson's habit of dismissing charges against men whom the troops had gone to great trouble to help in apprehending and bringing into court. In one instance, Dudley reported, Wilson acquitted a man of larceny but made him pay court costs and return the property he had stolen. For the sheriff and the army alike, such caprice destroyed all incentive to try to run down criminals.[17]

For other reasons, too, the army proved less effective than Wallace had hoped. The instructions governing the troops left considerable uncertainty about how large a role they could play in restoring order, but commanders preferred the narrowest possible interpretation. In practice, they generally acted only on the request and in the presence of a civil officer. When one of Dudley's subordinates helped a constable arrest the principals in a knife-wielding drunken brawl, the issue arose of which civil officers to assist. Wallace argued that the Secretary of

War's original orders permitted a comprehensive definition—territorial, county, and township. Again General Sherman thwarted the governor, and the army stuck to a limited interpretation. Only federal marshals and county sheriffs, or their deputies, would be aided. As the U.S. marshal refused to name a deputy in Lincoln County until peace was restored, that left Sheriff George Peppin, and he had all but abdicated months earlier.[18]

Still, Wallace procrastinated. He worked on *Ben-Hur* and, early in February 1879, journeyed to Colorado to meet his wife Susan and son Henry and conduct them back to Santa Fe.[19] Pressures mounted for him to visit Lincoln. One respected Santa Fean wrote from Fort Stanton that "nothing but a personal visit and a stay of some week or ten days, will enable you to form a correct idea of the true standing & bearing of the matter."[20] The governor, however, had already decided that April would be soon enough, and he had arranged with Judge Bristol to accompany him when he held the spring term of district court in Lincoln—*if* he thought he could safely preside in Lincoln.[21]

Late in February, however, events boiled over in Lincoln that altered the timetable. Ever since November, Huston Chapman and Susan McSween had kept up an almost hysterical agitation. Directed chiefly at Colonel Dudley, it also revived all the smoldering animosities of the Dolan-McSween feud and soon had the community in an uproar. Heartily sick of bloodshed, some of the leaders of the old warring factions got together on the night of February 18 to conclude a peace pact. Afterward, they staged a drunken celebration and, staggering down the street, came upon Huston Chapman. In the midst of an exchange of insults, one of the celebrants pressed a pistol against Chapman's breast and fired, killing him instantly.[22]

The senseless slaying of Chapman, dramatizing the gathering of some of the most violent of the old feudists, terrified Lincoln's citizens. In a climate of near public panic, the new sheriff, George Kimball, called for military help. Colonel Dudley sent a detachment to town to give visible reassurance. No further eruption occurred, and in a well-attended public meeting the people voiced a new-found appreciation for Dudley.[23]

In Governor Wallace, the Chapman killing and its aftermath stirred a bewildering ambivalence. He branded Colonel Dudley's dispatch of troops a "ridiculous action" that was likely to alarm the populace unnecessarily, but he then notified Colonel Hatch that conditions in Lincoln County might be so bad as to require "the instant proclamation of martial law." At the same time, the governor submitted to Secretary Schurz a "plan of campaign" that looked to the federal courts instead of military commissions to suppress outlawry, and he told Hatch that he hoped for a civil rather than a military solution. In one way, however, the Chapman affair produced a positive result. Although uncertain of the remedy, Wallace would procrastinate no longer in seeking one. He would go to Lincoln himself.[24]

Wallace reached his destination on March 5, 1879. He had traveled from Santa Fe with Colonel Hatch, who took his station at Fort Stanton while the governor established himself in rooms in Lincoln provided by merchant José Montaño. At once Wallace began talking with prominent citizens, especially Justice of the Peace Wilson, and acquainting himself with issues and personalities.

The governor's first priority was to get rid of Colonel Dudley. He had tried and failed in December, and he had spoken to Hatch about it several times since. On the eve of their departure from Santa Fe, Hatch had warned his superiors to expect another official request, this one not to be easily brushed aside.[25] The two men undoubtedly worked out the details during the journey to Lincoln.

What Wallace learned from Lincoln residents only fortified his resolve. Although they had just held a public meeting to pour out their gratitude to Dudley, Wallace had no trouble in finding men to accuse the colonel of favoritism toward the Dolan faction, of causing McSween's death, of contributing somehow to Chapman's murder, and of intimidating citizens from testifying in court or serving as jurors. That people believed these allegations, whether true or not, Wallace thought sufficient to unfit Dudley for his post. Besides, now that Wallace had taken personal charge of the effort to restore law and order, he had to have a commanding officer at Fort Stanton with whom he could work harmoniously.

On March 7 Wallace put these thoughts to paper for Colonel Hatch and concluded with an official request for Dudley's relief. Next day, to a predictable and not altogether unjustified explosion of rage, Hatch relieved Dudley. The post fell by seniority to Captain Henry Carroll, a steady veteran of modest ability, temperate habits, and honest disposition who had risen from the ranks to become a respected company officer. With what had to be a sense of personal vengeance as well as official satisfaction, Wallace returned to Lincoln from Fort Stanton on the night of March 8, called a public meeting, and claimed for himself the best day's work anyone had ever done in behalf of Lincoln County.[26]

With Dudley out of the way and Fort Stanton in the hands of an officer cheerfully responsive to Wallace's every wish, the governor concentrated on his central task—to purge the county of bad men. He hoped to accomplish this by arresting and trying all he could catch and driving the rest out by their example. One measure he pressed on Captain Carroll was simply to arrest everyone herding cattle who could not prove ownership by registered brand or bill of sale. But the main goal was to round up the outlaws who had terrorized the county for a year. From informants in Lincoln, he learned who the worst offenders were, and on March 11 he furnished Carroll with a list of thirty-five men to be sought out and arrested. "Push the 'Black Knights' without rest," he urged, "and regardless of boundary lines."[27]

Even before Colonel Hatch left for El Paso on March 11, Wallace had snared the fugitives he most wanted. These were four men directly implicated in the Chapman murder. Two were notorious outlaws, Jesse Evans and Billy Campbell, with the latter by all accounts the killer of Chapman. The others were Jimmy Dolan, leader of the old anti-McSween faction, and his chief henchman, Jacob B. Mathews. Learning that they were at Fairview, Lawrence G. Murphy's old ranch thirty-five miles west of Lincoln, Wallace asked Hatch to send a detachment to seize three of the culprits. He exempted Dolan in the vain hope that "his larger money interest in the county . . . would make him pliant for use as a witness." With Campbell, Evans, and Mathews safely confined at Fort Stanton, Dolan promptly came to Lincoln to surrender and continue his four-month effort to ingratiate himself with the governor. Wallace took his parole on condition that he remain within the limits of Fort Stanton. When he violated parole, Wallace had him placed under close guard—though in the comfortable setting of the post library rather than in the cells that confined Campbell, Evans, and Mathews.[28]

To these four prisoners Captain Carroll now began to add others on the list supplied by Wallace. With methodical persistence, he kept his patrols scouring the country and rounding up leading fighters of the old McSween and Dolan factions as well as rustlers and other desperadoes who had rushed to Lincoln County when all pretence at law enforcement had collapsed after McSween's death. By the end of March Wallace had a dozen imprisoned, and a week later a correspondent of the *Mesilla Independent* observed that the Fort Stanton guardhouse had become "a 'Bastille' crowded with civil prisoners."[29]

With these men in custody, Wallace faced the same looming obstacle that had thwarted him from the first. Efficient military action could corral fugitives, but the civil machinery remained ineffective to dispose of them. The problem surfaced on March 6 with the arrest of Evans, Campbell, and Mathews. Hatch sent word to Wallace to make certain that the sheriff was at the fort to greet them with arrest warrants. But warrants could not be issued without supporting affidavits. "The truth is," Wallace confessed, "the people here are so intimidated that some days will have to [pass] before they can be screwed up to the point of making the necessary affidavits." The governor therefore had to take responsibility for requesting that the prisoners be confined without warrants. "Hold them I beg of you," he pleaded. "To let them go now is to lose everything at the beginning of the struggle."[30]

As Wallace knew, such a stratagem could only delay the legal process, and that not for long. Lincoln's only practicing attorney lost no time in signing up Evans, Campbell, and Mathews as clients, then instituting habeas corpus proceedings. Wallace made haste to instruct Justice of the Peace Wilson that he lacked the authority to issue writs of habeas corpus, but Judge Bristol had no such handicap, and he would be in Lincoln soon for the April term of district court.[31]

Wallace's eagerness for reliable witnesses led him into a bizarre compact with one of the most notorious fighters of the Lincoln County War—William H. Bonney, soon to become a national celebrity as Billy the Kid. After a preliminary exchange of letters, they met face to face in Squire Wilson's rude dwelling in Lincoln. Bonney had been indicted for the murder of Sheriff William Brady the previous April and so could not avail himself of Wallace's amnesty proclamation. He could, though, and he did, negotiate a deal with the governor. He had witnessed the murder of Chapman, and in exchange for his testimony Wallace would ensure that he was not prosecuted for the murder of Sheriff Brady. Later, in a carefully contrived "arrest," Sheriff Kimball took the Kid into custody. However dramatic, it was somewhat anticlimactic, for on March 18 Evans and Campbell had induced their guard to desert, and the three had put the Fort Stanton guardhouse far behind them.[32]

Although Bonney stood ready to testify, Wallace still needed more witnesses. He had hoped that the steady accumulation of bad men in the Fort Stanton lockup would begin to restore confidence, but it did not, especially after the escape of Evans and Campbell had dramatized the military's imperfections. "'Say nothing,' seems to be the policy," observed the *Mesilla Independent.* "The man who dares to raise his voice against the acts of murderers, or attempts to expose their crimes, at once becomes the mark for the assassin's bullet." Judge Bristol thought this attitude created a serious obstacle to resolving Lincoln County's problems through the civil courts. The people, he wrote to Wallace, "consider their lives would be in peril if they should disclose criminal acts," and, he conceded, "there seems some ground for their fears."[33]

To the witness problem Wallace added a growing dissatisfaction with the army. He and Captain Carroll got along well. "He appears to be the man for the place," Wallace informed Hatch. But on March 20 Captain George A. Purington returned from a leave of absence. He ranked Carroll, and Hatch assigned him to command. Post commander before Dudley, Purington had shown even more openly than Dudley a partiality for the Dolan faction, and Wallace considered him almost as objectionable as Dudley. Purington promptly confirmed Wallace's fears, finding somewhere in army regulations an excuse for resisting almost everything the governor wanted to do. "The military," Wallace complained to Schurz ten days after Purington's arrival, "do not enter heartily into the work requested of them."[34]

A partial answer was for the governor to organize his own army, and by the end of March he had the rudiments of a militia company in place. Ultimately, it numbered about thirty men, virtually all Hispanic and mostly former McSween supporters. Juan Patrón commanded as captain. An educated young man with engaging ways, respected by Anglos as well as by Hispanics, he served the governor efficiently and loyally. The militia did some useful service, but they were poor substitutes for the regulars. Critics labeled them the "Heel-flies" and, as Squire Wilson noted, they would "make fun of them Generaly when they meet them."[35]

At the end of March, Wallace's mounting troubles led him back to a familiar nostrum—martial law. He could get few witnesses, and the men held illegally at Fort Stanton seemed likely to go free on writs of habeas corpus. Under Purington, the army cooperated halfheartedly, if at all. Moreover, even if court met, hardly anyone untainted by old rivalries could be found to serve as grand and petit jurors. Virtually every man of competence, Wallace concluded, "is yet all alive with prejudices and partialities." In these circumstances, martial law seemed the only answer. Habeas corpus could be suspended and the drawbacks of civil court avoided by trying all offenders by military commission. On March 31, therefore, the governor appealed by telegraph to Secretary Schurz and President Hayes to proclaim martial law at once.[36]

Like previous petitions for a military solution, this one came to nothing. Within four days, in fact, Wallace was briskly moving toward a civil solution. On April 4 he advised Schurz that, if the approaching session of district court turned out to be a failure, there would then be no recourse save martial law. And on the same day, he wrote Judge Bristol urging the necessity for a spring term of court in Lincoln.[37]

Much depended on the quality and vigor of the prosecution. District Attorney William L. Rynerson, a notorious Dolan partisan, could not be counted on to push aggressively for conviction. Wallace cast about for more conscientious and impartial lawyers who might be employed temporarily to assist Rynerson. Lincoln attorney Sidney Wilson declined; he was too lucratively busy representing the Fort Stanton prisoners in habeas corpus proceedings. Wallace appealed to New Mexico Attorney General Henry L. Waldo, one of the territory's ablest lawyers, to take personal charge, but Waldo was occupied in preparing to represent Colonel Dudley in the court of inquiry ordered by the army. Finally, Wallace engaged Ira E. Leonard, a Las Vegas lawyer and former Missouri state judge. Leonard arrived in Lincoln early in April and at once assumed much of the burden borne by Wallace. Their association turned out to be congenial and productive.[38]

Wallace greeted Judge Bristol and other officers of the district court when they arrived at Fort Stanton on April 13, but he did not remain for the session. He left for Santa Fe on April 18, ostensibly because he needed to prepare himself to testify in the forthcoming Dudley court of inquiry. That explanation rings somewhat hollow. It may simply have been an excuse, or rationalization, to get out of Lincoln. He had been there through six weeks of tiring, exasperating, and even dangerous labor, and he doubtless yearned to get back to his writing desk in Santa Fe.[39]

Court did not go well in his absence. Even before his departure, Bristol freed some of the Fort Stanton prisoners on writs of habeas corpus. Predictably, Rynerson failed to press the defendants, even with Leonard at his side. "I tell you Gov," Leonard wrote, "the prosecuting officer of this Dist is no friend to the enforcement of the law." Weak, timid, and fearful of assassination, Judge Bristol showed more interest in hurrying toward adjournment than in seeing justice done. The grand jury, composed of McSween adherents, returned two hundred indictments, principally against Dolan adherents. Most of the accused pleaded Wallace's amnesty proclamation and were promptly discharged. The few who declined to take this way out obtained a change of venue to Mesilla or Socorro. Of these, only one could not win acquittal when tried later. Although honoring his promise to testify before the grand jury in the Chapman murder, Billy Bonney found Bristol and Rynerson determined to thwart the bargain that he had struck with the governor. A year and a half later, the Kid heard Bristol sentence him to hang for the murder of Sheriff Brady.[40]

Almost no one seemed to think the court term a success. Captain Purington groused about the partisan grand jury and their favored treatment of the Kid and other McSween followers. Ira Leonard complained not only about Rynerson but more and more stridently about Bristol. This turned out to be a not wholly disinterested opinion, for a campaign soon developed, in which Wallace participated, to induce President Hayes to dismiss Bristol and to appoint Leonard in his place. The press, too, pronounced the session a failure, although the *Mesilla Independent* voiced the hopes of everyone by concluding that "feeling in Lincoln will perhaps cool down now."[41]

Actually it did, although the Dudley court of inquiry, played out at Fort Stanton through May and June 1879, kept interest in issues and personalities high. Governor Wallace came down from Santa Fe to testify as the first witness. He did not make a good showing, and Dudley's counsel, Attorney General Waldo, had no difficulty in exposing the weaknesses and contradictions in his testimony while also attacking the governor's motives with devastating effect.[42]

But Lincoln County did "cool down"—a relative term for that wild and violent part of the territory. And in the absence of any lurid new sensations to attract public attention, Wallace stepped forward with the only voice willing to pronounce the court term in Lincoln a success. As with his proclamation of November 1878, in need of success, he simply declared success. The Dolan and McSween factions were dead, he informed Schurz on June 11. The amnesty proclamation had produced exactly the desired effect: "to shear the past close off." Had all the men indicted stood trial, he reasoned, the court battles would have been accompanied by "heart burnings, disputes, revivals of old feuds, fights, shootings, bush-whackings, and general turmoil." As it was, most pleaded the governor's pardon, and the old hostilities had been put to rest. Outlaw gangs remained, he conceded. Most citizens favored eliminating them through martial law. But Wallace ticked off half a dozen reasons for resisting such a measure and trusting instead to the civil courts. At last, and finally, he had discarded this panacea for the territory's troubles.[43]

In fact, the governor's claim of success coincided with the end of the Lincoln County War. The war's end did not mark the return of peace. The gangs of which Wallace complained yielded only gradually to the restoration of law enforcement, as did old and deeply ingrained habits of looking to Winchester and Colt for the settlement of disputes. For a decade the county suffered more or less from crime and disorder. Also, the old factional rivalries left wounds that, as Wallace had predicted, took years to heal. But the danger of a resumption of open warfare between the Dolan and McSween factions, so imminent in the wake of the Chapman murder, subsided through the spring of 1879 and thus signaled, somewhat uncertainly, the close of the war.

Lew Wallace contributed to this result meagerly and only after indefensible delay. For five and a half months after taking office, he pursued an erratic course. He had no firm and consistent approach to the problem that he had been sent to New Mexico to solve. He made policy as he went along, and that not very thoughtfully.

His troubles began with his procrastination in going to the scene of the trouble and investigating in person. They continued with his vacillation over martial law; his abrupt and repeated shifts on this issue must have led President Hayes and Secretary of the Interior Schurz to the conclusion that the governor did not know what to do. The amnesty proclamation made matters worse. It proclaimed a peace that did not exist and pardoned the criminals responsible for the war. The declaration of peace not only raised false hopes but confused the army's role by appearing to cancel the very condition—the "insurrection" proclaimed by the President—that gave it legal legitimacy. The amnesty encouraged the return of criminals who had fled and made the governor's subsequent campaign to bring them to justice futile in all ways save as a demonstration of purpose.

And herein lay Wallace's sole constructive contribution to closing down the Lincoln County War. By spending six weeks in Lincoln, by demonstrating personal concern and leadership, and by aggressively attacking the outlaws with the army and his own militia, he helped in reviving the institutions of government and in reawakening the confidence of the people in them. That he did finally help bring about a resolution, however, does not excuse his failure to do more and to do it sooner.

What he should have done was to go to Lincoln at once and devise a plan of action on the scene. There he probably would not have issued his proclamation of peace and amnesty, and he probably would have pressed strenuously for martial law. There he would have seen the army in its congressionally imposed shackles, the sheriff helplessly barricaded at Fort Stanton, the courts powerless, the people demor- alized and unable to make legal process work, and murder, larceny, rape, and other crimes rampant across the land. As he had sensed at first, such extreme affliction called for an extreme remedy: martial law. By suspending the usual constitutional safeguards and trying forty or fifty of the chief troublemakers by military commission, Wallace might well have achieved quick and lasting victory. Colonel Dudley would have had to go, as he ultimately did, but by early March the army was already casting about for an officer with the "prudence and intelligence" to take his place in the event of martial law.[44]

Instead of unequivocally pressing for martial law, Wallace muddled through, and eventually the problem, with a slight boost from him, simply went away. Whether a firm and unswerving demand would have moved President Hayes cannot be known. Wallace never forced him to face up to the decision. By vacillating between military and civil approaches, Wallace gave the President and his advisers the excuse they wanted for avoiding such a politically distasteful remedy as martial law.

Wallace's erratic course seems understandable only in terms of that knight of chariot and galley, Judah Ben-Hur. Ever the romantic, the novelist found the mythical adventures of his biblical hero far more engrossing than the ugly reality of Lincoln County. Never was he happier than when lost in *Ben-Hur*, he wrote to his wife, "a perfect retreat from the annoyances of daily life as they are spun for me by enemies, and friends who might as well be enemies." Eagerly, he anticipated the words "The End"—"how beautiful they will look to me!"[45]

He wrote "The End" early in 1880. In April, he journeyed to New York to arrange publication. *Ben-Hur: A Tale of the Christ* appeared near the end of the year. Ultimately, *Ben-Hur* made Wallace a wealthy and revered literary figure. More immediately, it won him release from the oppressive post in New Mexico. President James A. Garfield, an old Shiloh comrade, found the tale of Ben-Hur so moving that he gave Wallace the post of minister to the court of the Turkish sultan in Constantinople, an appropriate reward for one who so treasured exotic peoples and places. On May 30, 1881, surely without regret, the governor who had arrived in Santa Fe on a springless buckboard climbed aboard a Pullman sleeper and turned toward new adventures and new realms to conquer.

Abbreviations

AAG	Assistant Adjutant General
AAAG	Acting Assistant Adjutant General
CO	Commanding Officer
DFRC	Denver Federal Records Center
DM	Department of the Missouri
DNM	District of New Mexico
HHC	J. Evetts Haley History Center, Midland, Texas
HL	Huntington Library, San Marino, California
IHS	Indiana Historical Society, Indianapolis
LR	Letters Received
LS	Letters Sent
M	National Archives Microfilm Publication
NARS	National Archives and Records Service, Washington, D.C.
NMSRCA	New Mexico State Records Center and Archives, Santa Fe
RG	Record Group
TANM	Territorial Archives of New Mexico
UAL	University of Arizona Library, Tucson

Notes

1 Alexander McSween

1. Marion Turner to Ed., Roswell, April 18, 1878, *Las Vegas Gazette*, May 4, 1878. Marion Turner assuredly did not write this literate and perceptive letter. From original documents known to be of his authorship, it is clear that Turner verged on illiteracy. Most likely it was written for Turner by Marshall A. (Ash) Upson, Roswell postmaster and sometime journalist who later ghosted Pat Garrett's history of Billy the Kid.

McSween gave his age as twenty-nine on his 1873 marriage certificate, which would have made 1844 his year of birth. However, church records in his birthplace, Prince Edward Island, give his date of birth as June 15, 1837, according to information obtained by Donald Lavash, historian at the New Mexico State Records Commission and Archives, from the Museum and Heritage Foundation of Prince Edward Island.

2. Carlota Baca Brent, interview with Frances E. Totty, December 6, 1937, WPA Files, Folder 212, NMSRCA.

3. A good picture of Lincoln County emerges from the Censuses of 1870 and 1880, NMSRCA.

4. Lawrence G. Murphy richly merits a serious biography, for he was a significant and colorful figure in New Mexico's territorial history. This sketch has been drawn in part from his obituary in the *Weekly New Mexican* (Santa Fe), October 26, 1878; from biographical notes compiled by Robert N. Mullin in the Mullin Collection, HHC; and from Philip J. Rasch, "The Rise of the House of Murphy," Denver Westerners, *Brand Book* 12 (1956), pp. 53–84. An excellent characterization by one who knew him is in Lily Klasner, *My Girlhood among Outlaws*, ed. Eve Ball (Tucson: University of Arizona Press, 1972), p. 94.

5. Deposition of George Van Sickle, June 12. 1878, in Frank Warner Angel, "Report on the Death of John H. Tunstall," Department of Justice,

1878. The Angel Report (hereafter cited as such) is in the Records of the Department of Justice in the National Archives. I have used a xerox copy in the Victor Westphall Collection, NMSRCA. Murphy's business activities, financial transactions, and land dealings may be partially traced in his ledger books for 1871 and 1872, Special Collections, UAL; and in Lincoln County Record Book A, a sort of catchall for transactions in the county that needed to be recorded in the early 1870s, kept at the county courthouse in Carrizozo, N.M. Murphy first operated from the post trader's store at Fort Stanton. Expelled from the fort in 1873, he built a large two-story building on the west edge of Lincoln.

6. Klasner, *My Girlhood among Outlaws,* p. 94. See also biographical notes in the Mullin Collection, HHC.

7. Frank Coe, interview with J. Evetts Haley, San Patricio, N.M., August 14, 1927, HHC.

8. *Daily New Mexican* (Santa Fe), November 20, 1876.

9. William Wier, interview with J. Evetts Haley, Monument, N.M., June 22, 1937, Vandale Collection 2H482, Barker History Center, University of Texas, Austin. Tunstall's voluminous letters to his family in England are remarkably revealing of Tunstall the man and entrepreneur. Typescripts are in the Maurice Garland Fulton Collection, UAL. They contain little that is not included in the published version: Frederick Nolan, ed., *The Life and Death of John Henry Tunstall* (Albuquerque: University of New Mexico Press, 1965). Fulton copied the originals and returned them to the family. Nolan worked from originals in possession of the family.

10. Tunstall to family, March 12 and April 27, 1877, in Nolan, *Life and Death of Tunstall,* pp. 201, 213.

11. For Chisum, see Harwood P. Hinton, "John Simpson Chisum, 1877–84," *New Mexico Historical Review* 31 (July 1956), pp. 177–205; (October 1956), pp. 310–37; and (January 1957), pp. 53–65. Hinton is working on a full-scale biography of Chisum.

12. "S" to Editor, May 31, 1878, *Grant County Herald* (Silver City), June 8, 1878. The interpretation in this paragraph needs no more documentation than Tunstall's letters home, which clearly and unmistakably spell out his objective and his methods.

13. Nolan, *Life and Death of Tunstall,* pp. 209, 214.

14. Notes on the Tunstall ranch and inventory of the Tunstall estate by Sam Corbet, n.d., both in Mullin Collection, Research Files, HHC. See also Huston I. Chapman to John Partridge Tunstall, Las Vegas, N.M., February 10, 1879, in Nolan, *Life and Death of Tunstall,* pp. 396–97. Chapman was Susan's attorney, aiding her in her capacity as administratrix of the Tunstall estate. The cows belonged to the widow Ellen Casey, whose assets were seized to satisfy a legal judgment against her. Tunstall wrote home on

May 7, 1877, saying he was about to get five thousand dollars worth of cattle for less than thirteen hundred dollars. Ibid., p. 216. See also notes based on the legal documents relating to the judgment and sale in the Casey biographical notes of the Mullin Collection, together with notes on the Tunstall cattle in notebook labeled "Lincoln County War," also in the Mullin Collection, HHC.

15. For the post tradership and the grain notes, see Nolan, *Life and Death of Tunstall,* pp. 224, 245. For the attack on Agent Frederick C. Godfroy, see McSween to Schurz, February 13, 1878, and McSween to Lowrie, February 25, 1878, RG 75, NARS, Office of Indian Affairs, LR, M234, Reel 576. For agency affairs, as well as much valuable data on Lincoln County events and personalities, see Lawrence L. Mehren, "A History of the Mescalero Apache Reservation, 1869–1881" (Master's Thesis, University of Arizona, 1968).

16. Affidavit of Andrew Boyle, June 17, 1878, Report of Inspector E. C. Watkins, No. 1981, June 27, 1878. RG 75, Records of the Bureau of Indian Affairs, Inspectors' Reports, 1873–80, NARS.

17. George Coe, interview with J. Evetts Haley, Ruidoso, N.M., June 12, 1939, HHC.

18. *Daily New Mexican* (Santa Fe), April 18, 1877. A photocopy of the articles of copartnership, March 14, 1877, is in the Fulton Collection, Box 12, Folder 3, UAL. Murphy divided his time between his ranch, Fairview, and Lincoln, where he continued to live at the Dolan store.

19. Photocopy of mortgage deed, January 19, 1878, in Fulton Collection, Box 12, Folder 4, UAL. The mortgage, to Santa Fe attorney Thomas B. Catron, covered all House real estate and improvements, merchandise, accounts receivable, fifteen hundred head of cattle, thirty-five horses, and twelve mules. Catron lent the partners twenty-five thousand dollars. If they defaulted, he could sell all the mortgaged property.

20. For Evans, see Philip J. Rasch, "The Story of Jessie Evans," *Panhandle Plains Historical Review* 33 (1960), pp. 108–21; and Grady E. McCreight and James H. Powell, *Jessie Evans: Lincoln County Badman* (College Station, Texas: Creative Publishing Co., 1983). Albert J. Fountain, Mesilla attorney and editor-publisher of the *Mesilla Valley Independent,* one of the best contemporary reporters of Lincoln County events, wrote that the Evans gang were "in the employ of certain persons who had contracts to supply the government with beef cattle, and that the cattle stolen from the citizens by the outlaws were turned into the government on these contracts." *Independent,* April 27, 1878.

21. After escaping, The Boys went to Brewer's ranch, obtained breakfast and mounts, and fled. Brewer is said to have had the horses ready and arranged to be conveniently absent when they showed up. See affidavits of Evans, June 14, 1878, and Andrew Boyle, June 17, 1878, in Report of Inspector E.

C. Watkins, No. 1981, June 27, 1878. RG 75, NARS, Records of the Bureau of Indian Affairs, Inspectors' Reports, 1873–80. An account of how Brewer went about this scheme, plausibly specific, appeared in a letter dated Río Pecos, April 8, 1878, signed "Cow-boy," who may have been Boyle. *Weekly New Mexican* (Santa Fe), April 20, 1878. Other sources bearing on the escape are "Lincoln" to Ed., November 20 and December 3, 1877, in *Mesilla Valley Independent*, November 24 and December 15, 1877; and, for McSween's version, his deposition in the Angel Report, cited in n. 5.

22. For Bristol, see Mullin Biographical Notes, HHC, and [William G. Ritch], Biographical Sketch concerning Warren Bristol, January 29, 1882, Ritch Collection, HL. For Rynerson, see Darlis A. Miller, "William Logan Rynerson in New Mexico, 1862–1893," *New Mexico Historical Review* 48 (April 1973), pp. 101–31; William G. Ritch, Biographical Sketch of William Logan Rynerson, n.d. [1882], Ritch Collection, HL; and Mullin Biographical Notes, HHC. For Brady, see Donald Lavash, *Sheriff William Brady: Tragic Hero of the Lincoln County War* (Santa Fe: Sunstone Press, 1986).

23. Affidavit of Emilie Scholand, Mesilla, December 23, 1877, Lincoln County, District Court, Civil Case No. 141, Fritz and Scholand v. McSween: assumpsit. Arrest warrant, same date. NMSRCA. Depositions of McSween and Dolan, Angel Report. The principal source for the complex story of the Fritz estate is McSween's deposition, June 6, 1878, in the Angel Report. Many of the legal documents in the case are annexed to this deposition as exhibits. Also of value are the deposition of David P. Shield, McSween's law partner and brother-in-law, Las Vegas, June 11, 1878, and Dolan's deposition, June 25, 1878, both in the Angel Report. McSween wrote an informative letter of explanation, January 10, 1878, which was printed in *Eco del Rio Grande* (Las Cruces), January 24, 1878. Voluminous as these sources are, they leave unanswered questions, including whether McSween may in fact have intended to abscond. Seven thousand dollars, the amount of the policy remaining after deduction of the fees of the bankers and lawyers who made the collection, seems hardly sufficient to have tempted him away from the wealth he hoped to gain from the association with Tunstall. Another possibility is that McSween foresaw violence and bloodshed, wanted no part of it, and planned to scout other opportunities before deciding whether to come back or not.

24. *Mesilla Valley Independent*, February 9, 1878. Civil Case No. 141, document file, as cited in n. 23, above. McSween and Dolan depositions, Angel Report.

25. The legal documents are in Lincoln County, District Court, Civil Case No. 141, Fritz and Scholand v. McSween: assumpsit. NMSRCA. The writ of attachment bears a notation indicating that it was retrieved from the body of Sheriff Brady after his murder. In addition, see Tunstall's account in

Nolan, *Life and Death of Tunstall*, p. 267; and depositions of McSween, June 6, 1878; Dolan, June 25, 1878; James Longwill, May 14, 1878; and Adolph P. Barrier, June 11, 1878, in Angel Report. Barrier gives the most detailed account and the only chronology that can be reconciled with the dates on the legal documents.

26. So Bristol declared in his charge to the grand jury at the April term of district court in Lincoln. The charge is reproduced verbatim in a supplement to the *Mesilla Valley Independent*, April 20, 1878. Bristol repeated the statement in a hearing on July 2, 1878, in Mesilla. *Mesilla News*, July 6, 1878. James Longwill, a Dolan associate who was present at the February hearing, also declared that Tunstall testified to the partnership in Mesilla. Longwill deposition, May 14, 1878, Angel Report. Both David P. Shield and Deputy Barrier, who were present at the hearing, swore that no such testimony was offered by either Tunstall or McSween. Undated deposition sworn by Shield and Barrier, Las Vegas, Angel Report. McSween explained in his deposition for Angel that articles of partnership were to be signed in May 1878 under terms that had already been negotiated. In fact, bank records disclose that the finances of the two had become so intertwined that no one could be blamed for believing they were already partners.

27. Depositions of McSween, June 6, 1878, and Barrier, June 11, 1878, Angel Report. The bond, with Rynerson's disapproving endorsement, is an exhibit appended to McSween's deposition.

28. Of the direct witnesses to the shooting, only Jesse Evans survived, and he denied being present. Most of what is known is contained in the depositions included in the Angel Report. See also Brady to Rynerson, March 5, 1878, in *Mesilla Valley Independent*, March 30, 1878; and "Stanton" to Ed., Fort Stanton, April 1, 1878, *Cimarron News and Press*, April 11, 1878. "Stanton" was McSween.

29. The usual version has the men gathering in response to news of Tunstall's death, but the timing hardly allows for these scattered people to have learned of the killing and ridden to Lincoln. James Longwill, one of Brady's men occupying the Tunstall store next door under the attachment writ, stated that the men collected before it was known that Tunstall had been shot. Deposition of Longwill, May 14, 1878, in Angel Report. Capt. George A. Purington, commanding officer at Fort Stanton, observed these men during a visit to McSween's home on February 21. Later he said that they were men of bad character and that McSween told him they were in his employ, some for four dollars a day. Purington to Angel, Fort Stanton, June 25, 1878, Angel Report.

30. Widenmann to Purington, Fort Stanton, February 20, 1878, Angel Report. Widenmann testified (deposition, Angel Report) that he went to the fort on February 19 and spent the night in the quarters of Lt. Samuel S.

Pague, and that about 1:00 A.M. on the twentieth Captain Purington woke him with a letter signed by Lincoln citizens saying Evans was in town and asking troops for his arrest. On the strength of this, Widenmann officially requested military aid.

On November 21, 1877, a federal grand jury at Mesilla had indicted Evans, Frank Baker, Tom Hill, Nicholas Provencia, and George Davis for larceny, and on November 24 the case was continued, with arrest warrants to issue. U.S. District Court, Third Judicial District, Record Book, 1871–79, pp. 659, 663, RG 21, Records of the District Court of the United States, Territory of New Mexico, DFRC. When and why U.S. Marshal John Sherman deputized Widenmann and entrusted the warrants to him is not known. On December 3, 1877, less than two weeks after the case was continued, Sherman requested Col. Edward Hatch, commanding the District of New Mexico, to furnish a detail of soldiers to Sheriff Brady, who also held commission as deputy U.S. marshal, to aid in apprehending Evans and his fellow fugitives. Hatch authorized Purington to furnish the troops, and it was under this authority that Purington assigned a detachment to Widenmann on February 20. Sherman to Hatch, Santa Fe, December 3, 1877; 1st end., Loud to Purington, December 10, 1877; 2d end., Purington to Loud, March 14, 1878, RG 393, NARS, LR, Hq. DNM, M1088, Reel 30.

31. These events are amply documented, but the chronology and sequence are badly confused. Sources: depositions of McSween, Widenmann (2), Atanacio Martínez (2), James Longwill, William Bonney, John B. Wilson, Florencio Gonzales, and Lt. M. F. Goodwin, with annexed documents; endorsement of Capt. George A. Purington, March 14, 1878; and Purington to Angel, June 25, 1878, all in Angel Report. Also Purington to AAAG, DNM, Fort Stanton, February 21, 1878, RG 393, NARS, LR, Hq. DNM, M1088, Reel 32; affidavit of George W. Peppin (a Brady deputy in the Tunstall store), April 15, 1878, in Lincoln County, District Court, Civil Case No. 141, document file, NMSRCA; McSween's "Stanton" letter, April 1, 1878, in *Cimarron News and Press*, April 11, 1878; *Mesilla Valley Independent*, April 27, 1878; and *Weekly New Mexican* (Santa Fe), May 4, 1878.

32. Deposition of John B. Wilson, August 31, 1878, Exhibit 13 to McSween deposition, Angel Report.

33. Depositions of McSween and Barrier, Angel Report.

34. For the mortgage, see n. 19, above. For a biography of Catron, see Victor Westphall, *Thomas Benton Catron and His Era* (Tucson: University of Arizona Press, 1973).

35. Lee Scott Theisen, ed., "Frank Warner Angel's Notes on New Mexico Territory, 1878," *Arizona and the West* 18 (Winter 1976), pp. 340–41. In preparing Lew Wallace for the governorship of New Mexico, investigator Angel gave him pithy characterizations of the principal figures in the Lincoln

County War, and on the New Mexico scene generally, which Wallace jotted down in a pocket notebook, now in the Wallace Papers, IHS. This article reproduces those notes, with the editor's annotations. For Axtell, see also Calvin Horn, *New Mexico's Troubled Years: The Story of Early Territorial Governors* (Albuquerque: Horn and Wallace, 1963), pp. 193–97; [William G. Ritch], Biographical Notes concerning Samuel Beach Axtell, Ritch Collection, HL; and Mullin biographical notes, HHC.

36. On February 24, 1878, almost certainly in response to Dolan's appearance in Mesilla, District Attorney Rynerson wired Governor Axtell. He told of the "bogus charge" against Brady and the seizure of the Tunstall store and urged him to get the aid of U.S. troops. Axtell did so in a letter to Colonel Hatch on February 25. On February 28, at Fort Stanton, Sheriff Brady composed a message to Tom Catron, which was taken to Mesilla and telegraphed to Santa Fe. It described McSween's army and its defiance of the law, portrayed Brady as powerless to keep the peace, and asked Catron to see Axtell and get an order for the Fort Stanton troops to protect him in his duties. Catron took this communication to Axtell, who enclosed it with a telegram to President Hayes, March 4, asking for military assistance. On March 5 telegraphic orders from the Secretary of War started down the chain of command. These and other military documents bearing on the issue are in two sources: RG 393, NARS, LR, Hq. DNM, M1088, Reel 32; and RG 94, NARS; Adjutant General's Office, LR (Main Series), 1871–80, M666, Reels 397 and 398, which contain File 1405 AGO 1878, documents relating to civil disturbances in Lincoln County (hereafter cited as File 1405 AGO 1878, NARS).

37. The proclamation is Exhibit 16 to McSween's deposition in the Angel Report. J. H. Farmer had been elected justice of the peace in the 1876 election, but he had resigned, and on February 14, 1877, the county commission had appointed Wilson (who had held the office in the past) pending another election. Axtell's proclamation declared this appointment illegal and all actions of Wilson void. Actually, the appointment was entirely in accord with the 1876 act of the territorial legislature creating county commissions, but this act in turn contravened the New Mexico organic act, which required justices to be elected. Clouded though this issue is, certainly Axtell moved hastily in also declaring in the proclamation that Judge Bristol's court was the only legal source of writs and processes and Brady the only authority to execute them. Lincoln County had five other precincts, each with its own elected justice of the peace and constable. Also bearing on Axtell's Lincoln visit and proclamation are Montague R. Leverson to President Hayes, March 16, 1878; and deposition of David P. Shield, Las Vegas, June 11, 1878, both in the Angel Report. Widenmann's version is in a letter to Ed., Lincoln,

March 30, 1878, *Cimarron News and Press*, April 11, 1878. Axtell's account is in his response to Angel's "interrogatories," Angel Report.

38. *Mesilla Valley Independent*, March 16 and April 23, 1878. Fearing death, Morton posted a letter in Roswell to a Virginia acquaintance explaining the circumstances of his seizure. Dated March 8, the day before the killing, it was printed in ibid., April 13, 1878. *Weekly New Mexican* (Santa Fe), May 4, 1878. See also Morton material in Mullin biographical notes, HHC. Morton was chief of the Dolan cow camp on the Pecos, and Baker was a member of Jesse Evans's gang.

39. Francisco Trujillo, one of the Regulators' Hispanic contingent, was present at the meeting and flatly stated that McSween, seeking to avoid arrest, offered a reward for Brady's assassination. On the ride back to Lincoln, according to Trujillo, the group split up, with the Hispanics going to San Patricio because the Anglos did not want them to share in the killing of Brady, who had a Hispanic wife. Interview with Edith Crawford, San Patricio, N.M., May 10, 1937, WPA Files, Folder 212, NMSRCA. Citing "parties in Lincoln," the anti-McSween *Mesilla News*, June 8, 1878, charged McSween and Chisum with inciting the Regulators to murder Brady.

40. Affidavits that Lt. Col. Nathan A. M. Dudley caused to be sworn in November 1878 aimed specifically at destroying Susan's reputation; hence they must be used with great caution. However, they do tend to show what people believed about her. The strongest evidence supporting the above generalizations appears in these affidavits and in the testimony of some of the witnesses in the Dudley court of inquiry, especially the Bacas. The affidavits are Exhibits 6C through 12, Records Relating to the Dudley Inquiry (CQ 1284), RG 153, NARS, Judge Advocate General's Office (hereafter cited as Dudley Court Record). There is a microfilm copy in Special Collections, UAL, a copy of which I have used through the courtesy of Donald Lavash.

41. Much about these events must remain speculation. On April 4 Murphy alerted the military at Fort Stanton that rumor in Lincoln placed Bristol and his party in danger, and an escort was sent to meet him. The new commanding officer, Lt. Col. Nathan A. M. Dudley, believed the report, and so did Judge Bristol. See Murphy to CO Fort Stanton, April 4, 1878, Exhibit 77–3, Dudley Court Record, NARS, and Dudley to AAAG, DNM, May 4, 1878, File 1405 AGO 1878, NARS. For newspaper comment see *Mesilla News*, June 8, 1878.

42. Bristol's charge to the grand jury is printed verbatim in a supplement to the *Mesilla Valley Independent*, April 20, 1878. The two reports of the grand jury are given verbatim in ibid., May 4, 1878. For the record of the court's proceedings, see Lincoln County District Court Journal, 1875–79, April 1878 term, pp. 264–91; and associated case files, NMSRCA. Although free of the

criminal charge, McSween still faced the Fritz-Scholand civil suit for ten thousand dollars. Since Brady had never completed the attachment of McSween's property, Judge Bristol ordered the new sheriff to resume the process. Bristol's order is in Civil Case No. 141, document file.

43. McSween and B. H. Ellis to Secretary of War, April 26, 1878, File 1405 AGO 1878, NARS. This is the copy transmitted to the Secretary of War. Copies also went to the President, Secretary of the Interior, territorial governor, and the press, and so they may be consulted elsewhere as well, especially in the newspapers. The *Mesilla Valley Independent*, May 4, 1878, contains a copy, together with a "card to the public," April 23, in which Dolan and Riley give notice of closing the store. Murphy went to Fort Stanton on April 23 and asked for military protection. Murphy to Dudley, April 23, 1878, Exhibit 77–12, Dudley Court Record, NARS.

44. A photocopy of McNab's surety bond for his appointment as deputy constable, April 27, 1878, is in the Mullin Collection, Research Files, HHC. That he obtained his commission in San Patricio is speculation; but Wilson had not yet been reelected to his old post, from which Axtell had dismissed him, and the inference seems reasonable.

45. A revealing chronicle of Copeland's activities during the last week of April, featuring excitement, confusion, and heavy drinking, is in the report of a soldier detailed to aid him: Cpl. Thomas Dole to CO Fort Stanton, May 1, 1878, File 1405 AGO 1878, NARS. See also "J" to Ed., Lincoln, May 3, 1878, *Weekly New Mexican* (Santa Fe), May 18, 1878; and *Mesilla News*, May 18, 1878. Copeland told Dudley that Rynerson had not left warrants with him when court adjourned, but Rynerson vigorously denied this. Dudley to AAAG, DNM, May 25, 1878, Exhibit 77–21, Dudley Court Record, NARS.

46. Smith to Post Adjutant Fort Stanton, May 1, 1878, File 1405 1878. "Outsider" to Ed., Fort Stanton, May 1, 1878, *Mesilla Valley Independent*, May 11, 1878. "Van" to Ed., and "J" to Ed., both Lincoln, May 3, 1878, *Weekly New Mexican* (Santa Fe), May 18, 1878. George Coe, interview with J. Evetts Haley, Glencoe, N.M., August 14, 1927, and Frank Coe, interview with J. Evetts Haley, San Patricio, N.M., August 14, 1927, HHC.

47. Dudley to AAAG, DNM, Fort Stanton, May 4, 1878, with enclosures, File 1405 AGO 1878, NARS. These documents set forth events from the military perspective in great detail. The quotation is from Dudley to AAAG, DNM, Fort Stanton, May 11, 1876, ibid.

48. Dudley to AAAG, DNM, Fort Stanton, May 25, 1878, File 1405 AGO 1878, NARS. "S" to Ed., Silver City, May 31, 1878, *Grant County Herald* (Silver City), June 8, 1878.

49. The proclamation, with Axtell's notice to Copeland, May 28, 1878, is printed in the *Weekly New Mexican* (Santa Fe), June 1, 1878. For Peppin's appointment, see Executive Record Book No. 2, May 31, 1878, TANM,

Reel 21, Frame 502, May 31, 1878, NMSRCA. There is no evidence directly linking Dolan to this scheme. It is unlikely that Axtell conceived it alone, however, and Dolan's presence in Santa Fe makes him the logical author.

50. Catron to Axtell, May 30, 1878, and Axtell to Hatch, same date; Hatch to AAG, DM, June 1, 1878; Loud to CO Fort Stanton, June 1; endorsement by Brig. Gen. John Pope, June 7, 1878, all in File 1405 AGO 1878, NARS. For the cow camp raid, see Dudley to AAAG, DNM, Fort Stanton, May 25, 1878, with enclosures, ibid.; *Cimarron News and Press,* June 6, 1878; and *Mesilla News,* June 1 and 8, 1878.

51. For the Leverson letters and the British diplomatic initiative, see Nolan, *Life and Death of Tunstall.* Ealy's letters to Rep. Rush Clark of Pennsylvania, April 5 and May 3, 1878, are in File 1405 AGO 1878, NARS. For Ealy's other contributions to primary source material, see the Ealy Papers, UAL, and Norman J. Bender, ed., *Missionaries, Outlaws, and Indians: Taylor F. Ealy at Lincoln and Zuñi, 1878–1881* (Albuquerque: University of New Mexico Press, 1984). The Angel Report itself contains much of the background.

52. Philip J. Rasch, "John Kinney: King of the Rustlers," English Westerners, *Brand Book* 4 (October 1961), pp. 10–12.

53. *Mesilla News,* June 15, 1878. "Scrope" to Ed., Fort Stanton, June 18, 1878, and idem., Lincoln, June 22, 1878, both in *Mesilla News,* June 29, 1878. "Scrope" was probably Dolan himself. Andrew Boyle to Ira Bond, Lincoln, August 2, 1878, *Grant County Herald* (Silver City), August 24, 1878 (repeated from *Mesilla News*). Peppin to Dudley, Fort Stanton, June 18, 1878 (noon); Goodwin to Post Adjutant, Fort Stanton, June 19, 1878; Dudley to AAAG, DNM, Fort Stanton, June 22, 1878, all in File 1405 AGO 1878, NARS. Special Order 44, Hq. Fort Stanton, June 16 [sic., 18], 1878; Dudley to Axtell, Fort Stanton, June 20, 1878, Exhibits 77–34 and 77–28, Dudley Court Record, NARS. The warrants were transmitted to Peppin by U.S. Marshal John Sherman, June 14, 1878 (Exhibit 77–33, Dudley Court Record), ordering the arrest of nine of the Regulators involved in the Blazer's Mills fight on April 4 and their appearance before U.S. district court in Mesilla. On June 22, 1878, with none of the warrants having been served, the U.S. grand jury in Mesilla indicted those named in the warrants, and Judge Bristol, sitting as federal judge, issued alias warrants (that is, second warrants where the first had failed). U.S. District Court, Third Judicial District, Record Book 1871–79, Criminal Case 411, June 22, 1878, p. 687, RG 21, Records of the District Court of the United States, Territory of New Mexico, DFRC.

54. So reported George Washington, the ubiquitous black handyman who went along as cook. *Mesilla News,* July 6, 1878.

55. For the June 27 fight, see *Weekly New Mexican* (Santa Fe), July 6,

1878; *Mesilla News,* July 6, 1878; Andrew Boyle to Ira Bond, Lincoln, August 2, 1878, *Grant County Herald* (Silver City), August 24, 1878 (repeated from *Mesilla News*); "Julius" to Ed., Lincoln, June 27, 1878, *Mesilla News,* July 6, 1878 (Julius was probably Dolan); Affidavit of Peppin, Fort Stanton, June 27, 1878, and Dudley to AAAG, DNM, Fort Stanton, June 29, 1878, File 1405 AGO 1878, NARS. For the July 3 fight, see *Mesilla News,* July 13, 1878; Dudley to AAAG, DNM, Fort Stanton, July 6, 1878, File 1405 AGO 1878; and Capt. Thomas Blair to Dudley, July 12, 1878, original in Fulton Collection, Box 11, Folder 7, UAL. For the July 4 skirmish at Chisum's ranch, see *Weekly New Mexican* (Santa Fe), July 27, 1878, and George Coe, interview with J. Evetts Haley, Glencoe, N.M., March 20, 1927, HHC. The original warrant for McSween's arrest, executed June 29, 1878, in Wilson's virtually illegible handwriting, is in Fulton Collection, Box 12, Folder 2, UAL.

56. Loud to CO Fort Stanton, Santa Fe, June 25, 1878; Special Order 49, Fort Stanton, June 28, 1878, Exhibits 77–45 and 78–2, Dudley Court Record, NARS.

57. Sources for the events of July 15–19 are voluminous and contradictory. The richest is the Dudley Court Record, NARS. The best synthesis is Philip J. Rasch, "Five Days of Battle," Denver Westerners, *Brand Book* 11 (1955), pp. 295–323.

58. Mary Ealy to Maurice G. Fulton, December 7, 1927, Fulton Collection, Box 1, Folder 8, UAL. Mary Ealy was the wife of Rev. Taylor F. Ealy, who came to Lincoln in February at McSween's behest and lived in the McSween house until after the killing of Brady.

59. Walter Noble Burns to Susan Barber, February 18, 1926, and Susan Barber to Fulton, White Oaks, N.M., October 12, 1928, Fulton Collection, Box 1, Folder 4, UAL.

60. *Mesilla Valley Independent,* May 11, 1878. Angel used the same words in his report to the Attorney General.

2 Billy the Kid

1. The clearest account of the escape is to be found in the testimony of the Kid, José Chaves y Chaves, Andrew Boyle, and Joseph H. Nash in the Dudley Court Record, NARS.

2. A number of good general works deal with the process of mythmaking in the American West, including Billy the Kid, but two notable recent studies address only the Kid: Stephen Tatum, *Inventing Billy the Kid: Visions of the Outlaw in America, 1881–1981* (Albuquerque: University of New Mexico

Press, 1982); and Jon Tuska, *Billy the Kid: A Bio-Bibliography* (Westport, Conn.: Greenwood Press, 1983).

3. These characterizations come from contemporary newspaper descriptions in the *New York Sun,* December 27, 1880, and *Las Vegas Gazette,* December 28, 1880; and also from Frank Coe, interview with J. Evetts Haley, San Patricio, N.M., March 20, 1927, HHC.

4. Several diligent researchers have tracked Billy through public records and stripped away much of the myth. For his years before Lincoln, see Philip J. Rasch, "New Light on the Legend of Billy the Kid," *New Mexico Folklore Record* 7 (1952–53), pp. 1–5; Rasch and Robert N. Mullin, "Dim Trails: The Pursuit of the McCarty Family," ibid. 8 (1953–54), pp. 6–11; and Rasch, "A Man Named Antrim," Los Angeles Westerners, *Brand Book* 6 (1956), pp. 48–54. For reference to Henry Antrim stealing horses in the Mesilla Valley, see *Mesilla Valley Independent,* October 13, 1877. Jesse Evans and his gang were there in September, and there is evidence establishing some relationship between Evans and the Kid prior to their association in Lincoln County. (Cf. Deposition of Panteleón Gallegos, April 14, 1878, in Frank Warner Angel, "Report on the Death of John H. Tunstall," Department of Justice, 1878. Hereafter cited as Angel Report.) The Kid's arrival on the lower Pecos in October 1877, where he spent several weeks, is recorded by both Barbara Jones and Lily Casey Klasner, in Eve Ball, *Ma'am Jones of the Pecos* (Tucson: University of Arizona Press, 1969), chap. 17; and Lily Klasner, *My Girlhood among Outlaws,* ed. Eve Ball (Tucson: University of Arizona Press, 1972), pp. 169–71. Lily's mother, the widow Ellen Casey, was on her way to Texas with a herd of cows stolen from Tunstall. They were headed off before reaching the state line by a force of Tunstall gunmen under Richard Brewer and John Middleton. It is tempting to speculate that the Kid accompanied them back to the mountains and formed the friendships that led to his employment at the Tunstall ranch. The Kid's participation in the liberation of Jesse Evans from the Lincoln jail is established in Francisco Trujillo, interview with Edith Crawford, San Patricio, N.M., May 10, 1937, WPA Files, Folder 212, NMSRCA. Trujillo, who later rode with the Kid, encountered the escape party and lost his arms and saddle to the Kid. Although eighty-five at the time of the interview, his recollections of many of the incidents of the Lincoln County War contain too many verifiable specifics to be discounted.

5. Tunstall wrote copious letters to his family, most of which are reproduced or summarized in Frederick Nolan, ed., *The Life and Death of John Henry Tunstall* (Albuquerque: University of New Mexico Press, 1965). Middleton is described in a letter of November 29, 1877, found on p. 249.

6. Depositions of William H. Bonney, June 8, 1878, and Robert A. Widenmann, June 6, 1878, Angel Report. For data on the other Tunstall hands, see biographical notes in the Mullin Collection, HHC.

7. The best sources from which to reconstruct these events are the depositions in the Angel Report, all sworn within three to four months of Tunstall's death. There are more than twenty by participants on both sides. The ones most directly useful here are those of Robert A. Widenmann, June 6; Jacob B. Mathews, June 22; Panteleón Gallegos, April 14; Godfrey Gauss, June 6; John Middleton, June 13; and William H. Bonney, June 8. Morton and Hill were killed before they could give direct testimony, and Jesse Evans simply denied being present. Most likely, however, the three shot Tunstall down before giving him a chance to surrender. They probably reacted to opportunity rather than plan, animated by the expectation of Dolan's approval and perhaps even by a tangible reward. See also Philip J. Rasch, "Prelude to the Lincoln County War: The Murder of John Henry Tunstall," Los Angeles Westerners, *Brand Book* 7 (1957), pp. 78–95.

8. So Martínez confessed to Lt. Millard F. Goodwin, a military officer from Fort Stanton. Deposition of Goodwin, Angel Report.

9. The moves and countermoves of February 19–23, badly scrambled in most accounts, may be reconstructed from the following sources: depositions of McSween, Widenmann (2), Martínez (2), James Longwill, William Bonney, John B. Wilson, Florencio Gonzales, and Lt. M. F. Goodwin, with annexed documents; endorsement of Capt. George A. Purington, March 14, 1878; and Purington to Angel, June 25, 1878, all in the Angel Report. Also Purington to AAAG, DNM, Fort Stanton, February 21, 1878, RG 393, NARS, LR, Hq. DNM, M1088, Reel 32; affidavit of George W. Peppin (a Brady deputy), April 15, 1878, in Lincoln County, District Court, Civil Case No. 141, document file, NMSRCA; "Stanton" [McSween] to Ed., April 1, 1878, *Cimarron News and Press*, April 11, 1878; *Mesilla Valley Independent*, April 27, 1878; and *Weekly New Mexican* (Santa Fe), May 4, 1878.

10. Besides Bonney, alias Antrim and alias the Kid, the core group included at least the following men, perhaps others: Dick Brewer, Frank McNab, Josiah G. (Doc) Scurlock, Charles Bowdre, Fred Waite, John Middleton, Henry Brown, Jim French, the cousins Frank and George Coe, John Scroggins, and Steve Stevens.

11. Neither Dolan nor McSween had the money to pay daily wages to their gunmen. Many of Dolan's fighters, of course, already drew wages as employees of The House, but the Dolan-Riley mortgage of January 1878 placed The House on the threshold of bankruptcy, and in May the partners went into bankruptcy. The record of McSween's bank account at the First National Bank of Santa Fe (Archive 177, Special Collections, University of New Mexico Library, Albuquerque) shows McSween to have been equally insolvent at this time. Repeatedly throughout the winter of 1877–78 he overdrew his account.

12. *Mesilla Valley Independent*, March 16, April 13, and April 23, 1878.

Morton's letter is printed in the April 13 issue. *Weekly New Mexican* (Santa Fe), May 4, 1878. Morton biographical notes, Mullin Collection, HHC. For reminiscent accounts, none very satisfactory, see Francisco Trujillo, interview with Edith Crawford, San Patricio, N.M., May 10, 1937, WPA Files, Folder 212, NMSRCA; Frank Coe, interview with J. Evetts Haley, San Patricio, N.M., August 14, 1927, HHC; and Florencio Chaves, interview with J. Evetts Haley, Lincoln, N.M., August 15, 1927, HHC.

13. The basic facts are set forth in *Mesilla Valley Independent,* April 13, April 27, and May 4, 1878, and *Weekly New Mexican* (Santa Fe), May 4, 1878. Reminiscent accounts are Robert Brady (William's young son), interview with Edith L. Crawford, Carrizozo, N.M., c. 1937; Gorgonio Wilson (son of Justice of the Peace Wilson), interview with Edith Crawford, Roswell, N.M., 1938; and Carlota Baca Brent (daughter of Saturnino Baca), interview with Francis E. Totty, December 6, 1937, all in WPA Files, Folder 212, NMSRCA; Juan Peppin (son of George Peppin), interview with Maurice G. Fulton, Artesia, N.M., c. 1930, Mullin Collection, HHC. The conventional account has the Kid running out to steal Brady's rifle. More plausibly, he risked this dash for the arrest warrant. Frank Coe said that the Kid jumped the wall "and ran to get the papers from Brady." Interview with J. Evetts Haley, San Patricio, N.M., March 20, 1927, HHC. Billy probably failed in his mission, for Deputy Peppin served the warrant on McSween that afternoon. Also in Brady's pocket was the writ of attachment on McSween's property, issued by Judge Bristol. The original writ (Lincoln County, District Court, Civil Case No. 141, NMSRCA) bears a notation that it was retrieved from the body of Sheriff Brady. Besides Bonney and French, the members of the death squad were Frank McNab, John Middleton, Fred Waite, and Henry Brown. Rob Widenmann was also there—to feed Tunstall's dog, he later explained—and may have joined in the assassination. Thereafter, anti-McSween newspapers contemptuously called him "the dog-feeder."

14. Ealy and his wife Mary wrote several accounts of these experiences in the 1920s. They are in the Ealy Papers, Special Collections, UAL. Frank Coe said Corbet put French in the cellar under the kitchen of the Tunstall store, next door, and spread a carpet over the trapdoor. Interview with J. Evetts Haley, San Patricio, N.M., March 20, 1927, HHC.

15. The most direct testimony is by David M. Easton, an eyewitness, before the Dudley court of inquiry on June 7, 1879, Dudley Court Record, NARS. His account agrees with one in the *Mesilla Valley Independent,* April 13, 1878, and generally with the recollections of Frank Coe, interview with J. Evetts Haley, San Patricio, N.M., March 20 and August 14, 1927, HHC; and a comment by Coe, c. 1927, on the version given in Walter Noble Burns's *Saga of Billy the Kid,* Mullin Collection, HHC. Dr. Blazer's son, thirteen at the time and a witness, steadfastly maintained that firing broke

out without any preliminary conversation involving Coe, and that the Kid counted the shots from Roberts's rifle and after the sixth rushed to the doorway and fired the shot that downed Roberts. Blazer said that the Kid gave this version in words and pantomime at Blazer's Mills on the way to Lincoln after his trial in Mesilla in 1881. See A. N. Blazer to Maurice G. Fulton, Mescalero, N.M., April 24, 1931, and August 27, 1937, Fulton Collection, Box 1, Folder 7, UAL; and Paul A. Blazer [Dr. Blazer's grandson], "The Fight at Blazer's Mill: A Chapter in the Lincoln County War," *Arizona and the West* 6 (Autumn 1964), pp. 203–11. It should be noted in this connection that Easton said that Roberts told him before dying that Bowdre had shot him, and that Dr. Blazer was foreman of the grand jury that heard testimony and indicted Bowdre for the murder of Roberts. Besides those named in the text, participating Regulators were Doc Scurlock, Frank McNab, John Scroggins, "Dirty Steve" Stevens, Fred Waite, Henry Brown, and Jim French. There is some question whether Frank Coe was a member of the group or just happened to be there. See *Mesilla Valley Independent*, June 14, 1879. Ignacio Gonzales and Sam Smith arrived with the Regulators, but did not stop.

16. Lincoln County, District Court Journal, 1875–79, April 1878 term, pp. 264–91. NMSRCA. For the charge that the Regulators planned to waylay Judge Bristol and party, see *Mesilla Valley Independent*, April 13, 1878. The fear had enough substance for the commanding officer at Fort Stanton to send a military escort to meet him.

17. For newspaper accounts of the Battle of Lincoln, see *Weekly New Mexican* (Santa Fe), May 11, 1878; "El Gato" to Ed., Fort Stanton, May 10, 1878, ibid., June 1, 1878; "Van" to Ed., Lincoln, May 3, 1878, *Mesilla News*, May 18, 1878; and "Outsider" to Ed., Fort Stanton, May 1, 1878, *Mesilla Valley Independent*, May 11, 1878. "Outsider," whose account is the most reliable and objective, may have been Edgar A. Walz, brother-in-law of Thomas B. Catron, who held the mortgage on the Dolan-Riley property and had just foreclosed. He sent Walz to manage his property. Military sources are: Dudley to AAAG, DNM, Fort Stanton, May 4, 11, and 15, with enclosures (including Lieutenant Smith's informative report of May 1) in File 1405 AGO 1878, NARS. Frank and George Coe left detailed and graphic reminiscent accounts in interviews with J. Evetts Haley, HHC. Also, George Coe gives an account in his *Frontier Fighter: The Autobiography of George W. Coe*, with Nan Hillary Harrison (Boston: Houghton-Mifflin Company, 1934). The Haley interviews are much more useful than the book and are used here instead. The most recent edition of *Frontier Fighter* is a Lakeside Classics issue for Christmas 1984, edited by Doyce B. Nunis, Jr.

18. Deposition of Lt. M. F. Goodwin, June 24, 1878, Angel Report. Goodwin commanded the detail that arrested McSween in San Patricio,

which he dates on May 6. Military documents cited in n. 17, however, show that it was May 2.

19. A biographical sketch is Philip J. Rasch, Joseph E. Buckbee, and Karl K. Klein, "Man of Many Parts," English Westerners, *Brand Book* 5 (January 1963), pp. 9–12.

20. For press accounts, see *Mesilla News*, June 1, 1878; *Cimarron News and Press*, June 6, 1878; and *Weekly New Mexican* (Santa Fe), June 8, 1878. Miliary sources are Dudley to AAAG, DNM, Fort Stanton, May 25, 1878, enclosing Riley to Dudley, May 17 and 19, and Copeland to Thornton, May 24, File 1405 AGO 1878, NARS. Francisco Trujillo, who was present, said Bonney and Chaves killed "Indian." Interview with Edith Crawford, San Patricio, N.M., May 10, 1937, WPA Files, Folder 212, NMSRCA. "Indian" is variously named in the sources and identified both as part Navajo and as part Comanche. Most likely, his name was Manuel Segovia. Sheriff Copeland denied giving Scurlock and his men orders to seize the horses, and Colonel Dudley interpreted this to mean that Scurlock was not a deputy, which is not what Copeland said. Sources also designate Chaves a deputy. There seems little question that Copeland had deputized Scurlock and Chaves, even though he did not instruct them to take the horses. Another cover for the expedition was a probate court order to impound a horse belonging to the estate of Buck Morton, former boss of the Dolan cow camp killed by the Regulators in March. *Weekly New Mexican* (Santa Fe), June 1, 1878.

21. *Mesilla News*, June 15, 1878. "Scrope" to Ed., Fort Stanton, June 18, 1878, and same to same, Lincoln, June 22, 1878, both in *Mesilla News*, June 29, 1878. "Scrope" was probably Dolan himself. Andrew Boyle to Ira Bond, Lincoln, August 2, 1878, *Grant County Herald* (Silver City), August 24, 1878 (repeated from *Mesilla News*). Peppin to Dudley, Fort Stanton, June 18, 1878 (noon); Goodwin to Post Adjutant Fort Stanton, June 19, 1878; Dudley to AAAG, DNM, Fort Stanton, June 22, 1878, all in File 1405 AGO 1878, NARS. Special Order 44, Hq. Fort Stanton, June 16 [sic., 18], 1878; Dudley to Axtell, Fort Stanton, June 20, 1878, Exhibits 77–34 and 77–28, Dudley Court Record, NARS. The warrants were transmitted to Peppin by U.S. Marshal John Sherman, Santa Fe, June 14, 1878 (Exhibit 77–33, Dudley Court Record), ordering the arrest of nine of the Regulators involved in the Blazer's Mills fight and their appearance before U.S. district court in Mesilla. On June 22, 1878, with none of the warrants having been served, the U.S. grand jury in Mesilla indicted those named in the warrants, and Judge Bristol, sitting as federal judge, issued alias warrants (that is, second warrants where the first had failed). U.S. District Court, Third Judicial District, Record Book 1871–79, Criminal Case 411, June 22, 1878, p. 687, RG 21, Records of the District Court of the United States, Territory of New Mexico, DFRC.

22. *Weekly New Mexican* (Santa Fe), July 6, 1878. *Mesilla News*, July 6, 1878. "Julius" [probably Dolan] to Ed., Lincoln, June 27, 1878, ibid. Andrew Boyle to Ed., Lincoln, August 2, 1878, *Grant County Herald* (Silver City), August 24, 1878 (repeated from *Mesilla News*). Dudley to AAAG, DNM, Fort Stanton, June 29, 1878, with enclosure, affidavit of George W. Peppin, June 27, 1878; and Capt. Henry Carroll to Post Adjutant Fort Stanton, July 1, 1878, File 1405 AGO 1878, NARS. Special Order 48, Fort Stanton, June 27, 1878; Dudley to Carroll, Fort Stanton, June 27, 1878 (midnight); Special Order 49, Fort Stanton, June 28, 1878, Exhibits 77–43, 77–44, 78–2, Dudley Court Record, NARS. Fort Stanton Post Returns, June 1878, NARS, M617, Reel 1218. Francisco Trujillo, interview with Edith Crawford, May 10, 1937, WPA Files, Folder 212, NMSRCA.

23. *Mesilla News*, July 13, 1878. Andrew Boyle to Ed., Lincoln, August 2, 1878, *Grant County Herald*, August 24, 1878 (repeated from *Mesilla News*). George Coe, interview with J. Evetts Haley, Glencoe, N.M., March 20, 1927, HHC. Dudley to AAAG, DNM, Fort Stanton, July 6, 1878, with enclosures, File 1405 AGO 1878, NARS. Petition to Dudley, July 4, 1878, Exhibit 51, Dudley Court Record, NARS. Capt. Thomas Blair to Dudley, Fort Stanton, July 12, 1878, Fulton Collection, Box 11, Folder 7, UAL. This is the original of Blair's lengthy report of his investigation of the posse's excesses at San Patricio.

24. *Weekly New Mexican* (Santa Fe), July 27, 1878. George Coe, interviews with J. Evetts Haley, Glencoe, N.M., March 20, 1927, and Ruidoso, June 12, 1939, HHC.

25. Sources for the events of July 15–19 are voluminous and contradictory. The richest is the Dudley Court Record, NARS. The best synthesis is Philip J. Rasch, "Five Days of Battle," Denver Westerners, *Brand Book* 11 (1955), pp. 295–323.

26. Susan E. Barber, interview with J. Evetts Haley, White Oaks, N.M., August 16, 1927, HHC. In addition to those named above, the defenders were Harvey Morris (a luckless young Kansan reading law in McSween's office), Joseph Smith, Thomas Cullins, George Bowers, José Chaves y Chaves, Yginio Salazar, Ignacio Gonzales, Vicente Romero, Francisco Zamora, and José María Sánchez.

27. Dudley to AAAG, DNM, Fort Stanton, July 18, 1878, enclosing proceedings of a board of officers to investigate the firing on the soldier, July 17, File 1405 AGO 1878, NARS.

28. The bulk of the testimony and exhibits in the Dudley Court Record treat this matter.

29. The best sources for this affair are military records: Dudley to AAAG, DNM, Fort Stanton, August 3, 6, 7, 8, and 10, 1878, with enclosures, File 1405 AGO 1878, NARS. A rich source, enclosure to Dudley's of August 10,

is a lengthy report of an investigation by Capt. Thomas Blair which includes the accounts of Agent Godfroy, Dr. Blazer, and Interpreter José Carrillo. See also *Mesilla Independent*, August 15, 1878; and *Cimarron News and Press*, September 19, 1878. The Coes gave especially good reminiscent accounts: George Coe, interview with J. Evetts Haley, Glencoe, N.M., March 20, 1927; and Frank Coe, ibid., San Patricio, N.M., August 14, 1927, both in HHC.

30. For the whereabouts of the Kid and other prominent Regulators, see Dudley to AAAG, DNM, August 31, September 7 and 28, 1878, with enclosures, File 1405 AGO 1878, NARS; diary of Sallie Chisum, Chaves County Historical Society, Roswell, N.M., excerpts provided by Harwood P. Hinton; George Coe, interview with J. Evetts Haley, Glencoe, N.M., March 20, 1927, HHC; and Henry F. Hoyt, *A Frontier Doctor* (Boston: Houghton-Mifflin Company, 1929), pp. 91–94. These sources generally support the sequence traced in the usually unreliable Pat F. Garrett, *The Authentic Life of Billy the Kid* (Santa Fe: New Mexican, 1882), chap. 13. There have been many editions of this work, ghosted by Ash Upson. I have used the University of Oklahoma Press edition of 1954, which went into a twelfth printing in 1980.

31. Dudley to AAAG, DNM, Fort Stanton, September 28, 29 (2), and October 3, 1878, with enclosures, File 1405 AGO 1878, NARS. Frank Coe, interview with J. Evetts Haley, San Patricio, N.M., August 14, 1927, HHC. For a biography of Selman, see Leon C. Metz, *John Selman, Gunfighter*, 2d ed. (Norman: University of Oklahoma Press, 1980).

32. Proclamation of November 13, 1878, Executive Record Book No. 2, 1867–82, pp. 356–58, TANM, Reel 21, Frame 505, NMSRCA. It was printed in the territorial press; for an example, see *Mesilla Valley Independent*, November 23, 1878.

33. *Mesilla News*, March 1, 1879. *Las Vegas Gazette*, March 1, 1879. *Las Cruces Thirty-Four*, March 6 and 19, April 9, 1879. *Mesilla Valley Independent*, March 1 and 22, 1879. Dudley to AAAG, DNM, Fort Stanton, February 19, 1879, with enclosures, File 1405 AGO 1878, NARS. The most detailed and authoritative evidence is a newspaper account of the testimony of participants and witnesses in Judge Bristol's court in Mesilla in July 1879. *Mesilla Valley Independent*, July 5, 1879. Some accounts say Chapman's body was drenched with whiskey and set afire. I think it more likely, as the witnesses last cited agreed, that the pistol shot ignited his clothing. A reminiscent account by an eyewitness is Edgar A. Walz, "Retrospective," October 1931, Museum of New Mexico Library, Santa Fe. Walz was Thomas B. Catron's brother-in-law and agent in Lincoln. For a synthesis of the evidence, see Philip J. Rasch, "The Murder of Huston I. Chapman," Los Angeles Westerners, *Brand Book* 8 (1959), pp. 69–82.

34. Telegram, Wallace to Secretary of the Interior Carl Schurz, Santa Fe, October 5, 1879. Wallace Papers, IHS. I have used a microfilm version loaned by Donald Lavash.

35. Except for Bonney's opening letter, a photocopy of which is displayed at the state monument in Lincoln, the letters are in the Wallace Papers, IHS. For this story, see Philip J. Rasch, "The Governor Meets the Kid," *English Westerners, Brand Book* 8 (April 1966), pp. 5–12.

36. Notes by Wallace of his meeting with the Kid, March 29, 1879, Wallace Papers, IHS.

37. Wallace to Schurz, Lincoln, March 31, 1879. Wallace Papers, IHS.

38. *Indianapolis World,* June 8, 1902.

39. Ira E. Leonard to Wallace, Lincoln, April 28, 1878, Wallace Papers, IHS. For court actions, see Lincoln County, District Court Journal, 1875–79, April 1879 term, pp. 296–387, NMSRCA. *Mesilla Valley Independent,* May 10, 1879.

40. Both the warrant and the five hundred dollar reward, with the latter offered on December 13, 1880, are recorded in Executive Record Book No. 2, 1867–82, pp. 507–08 and 473, TANM, Reel 21, Frames 581 and 565, NMSRCA.

41. For these events see Leon C. Metz, *Pat Garrett: The Story of a Western Lawman* (Norman: University of Oklahoma Press, 1973), chaps. 3–9; and Philip J. Rasch, "The Hunting of Billy, the Kid," English Westerners, *Brand Book* 2 (January 1969), pp. 1–10.

3 Colonel Dudley

1. Much about Dudley, personally as well as professionally, is revealed by his military personnel file in the National Archives: 6674 ACP 1876, RG 94, Appointments, Commissions, and Promotions [ACP] Files. See also Philip J. Rasch, "The Trials of Lieutenant-Colonel Dudley," English Westerners, *Brand Book* 7 (January 1965), pp. 1–7; and Rasch, "The Men at Fort Stanton," ibid. 3 (April 1961), pp. 2–78.

2. The orders came down the chain of command by telegraph on March 5, 1878. File 1405 AGO 1878, NARS.

3. These tortuous proceedings are best reconstructed from Dudley's weekly reports, with enclosures, during May and June 1878 in File 1405 AGO 1878, NARS.

4. 20 Stat. 145–52 (June 18, 1878). See also Larry D. Ball, *The United States Marshals of New Mexico and Arizona Territories, 1846–1912* (Albuquerque: University of New Mexico Press, 1978), pp. 91–92.

5. Teleg., Loud to CO Fort Stanton, Hq. DNM, Santa Fe, June 25, 1878. Special Order 49, Fort Stanton, June 28, 1878. Exhibits 77–45 and 78–2, Dudley Court Record, NARS.

6. Dudley to AAAG, DNM, Fort Stanton, July 13 and 18, 1878, with enclosures, File 1405 AGO 1878, NARS.

7. Peppin to Dudley, Lincoln, July 16, 1878. Dudley to Peppin, Fort Stanton, same date. Exhibits 48 and 49, Dudley Court Record, NARS. Dudley to AAAG, DNM, Fort Stanton, July 18, 1878, File 1405 AGO 1878, NARS.

8. The report of the board, July 17, 1878, was an enclosure to Dudley to AAAG, DNM, Fort Stanton, July 18, 1878, which also contained much informative material, File 1405 AGO 1878, NARS. See also testimony of Capt. George A. Purington and Asst. Surgeon Daniel M. Appel, Dudley Court Record, NARS.

9. Dudley to AAAG, DNM, Fort Stanton, July 20, 1878, enclosing document dated July 18 and signed by Dudley, Purington, Appel, Capt. Thomas Blair, Lt. M. F. Goodwin, and Lt. S. S. Pague. See also testimony of Dudley, Purington, Appel, and Goodwin. Dudley Court Record, NARS.

10. Testimony of Lt. M. F. Goodwin (Dudley's adjutant on July 19), Dudley Court Record, NARS. Fort Stanton Post Returns, July 1878, NARS, M617, Reel 1218.

11. Dudley to AAAG, DNM, Fort Stanton, July 20, 1878, File 1405 AGO 1878, NARS. Affidavit of Deputy John Long, Fort Stanton, July 21, 1878, Mullin Collection, HHC. Testimony of Peppin, Purington, Appel, Goodwin, George Washington, José María Aguayo, and Pvt. James Bush; notes by Appel, July 20, 1878; affidavits of Peppin and Long, November 6 and 9, 1878, all in Dudley Court Record, NARS.

12. Testimony of Peppin, Dudley, Ellis, Purington, Goodwin, Sgt. Harlin Lusk, Sgt. Andrew Keefe, and Pvt. James Bush, Dudley Court Record, NARS. Dudley to AAAG, DNM, Fort Stanton, July 20, 1878, File 1405 AGO 1878, NARS.

13. Testimony of Purington, Goodwin, Appel, Peppin, Lusk, Washington, John B. Wilson, Theresa Phillipowski, Josefita Montaño, Martín Chaves, and Sgt. O. D. Kelsey, Dudley Court Record, NARS. Dudley to AAAG, DNM, Fort Stanton, July 20, 1878, File 1405 AGO 1878, NARS.

14. Testimony of Ellis, Washington, Chaves, Lusk, Bush, Peppin, Kelsey, Purington, Appel, and Samuel Corbet, Dudley Court Record, NARS. Sergeant Lusk and Private Bush testified, none too coherently, that Dudley sent Bush to alert Peppin to the withdrawal of these McSween men, and then criticized him for not coming soon enough to catch them. In his summation at the close of the court of inquiry, however, Dudley's counsel, Henry L. Waldo, effectively discredited this testimony.

15. Testimony of Washington, Phillipowski, Chaves, Corbet, Lusk, Kelsey, Keefe, Goodwin, Purington, Sebrian Bates, and Francisco Romero y Valencia, Dudley Court Record, NARS. Sergeant Keefe, who had charge of the Gatling gun, denied that it was ever aimed at the hills north of the river, but he was contradicted by all the other witnesses named. It is possible, however, that the McSween men retreated because of fire from the posse rather than because of the threat of the artillery. Martín Chaves, the only one of this group to testify, did not even see the artillery.

16. Fifteen witnesses, including Dudley and Wilson, gave their version of the conversation between them. Dudley Court Record, NARS. About half of them related the double ironing threat, while the other half denied that it had occurred. Because denial is easier than invention, and because the language is wholly consistent with Dudley's character, I believe that it happened. See also affidavit of Wilson, c. March 1879, Wallace Papers, IHS.

17. As with the exchange between Dudley and Wilson, a parade of witnesses, including Dudley and Susan, gave contradictory and partisan accounts of this conversation. The disagreement, however, was less of substance than tone. Susan and her friends accused Dudley of anger and rudeness. Dudley and his friends protested dignity and courtesy in the face of great provocation. Dudley Court Record.

18. Testimony of Peppin, Dudley Court Record, NARS. Affidavits of Peppin, November 6, 1878, and Deputy John Long, November 9, 1878, Exhibits 8 and 6C, ibid.

19. Testimony of Corbet, Peppin, Appel, Dudley, David M. Easton, Susan McSween, and M. L. Pierce, Dudley Court Record, NARS.

20. Two witnesses in the Dudley Court, Alexander Rudder and Samuel Beard, testified to overhearing a conversation between Dolan and Dudley at Fort Stanton on July 18, in which Dolan said that he had to have army help and Dudley promised to come down next day and give help. Over the years, several fanciful tales based on this allegation found their way into the memories of participants. Dudley denied the conversation, and his officers supported him. Dolan testified that he spent the afternoon of the eighteenth at the home of the post butcher, Charles McVeagh, three-fourths of a mile east of the fort and did not go to the fort at all. McVeagh confirmed this. In his summation, Dudley's counsel convincingly refuted the stories of Rudder and Beard, and, in fact, their testimony is flawed with inconsistencies and obscurities. Dudley Court Record.

21. So testified Sebrian Bates, the McSweens' servant, who admittedly was not a very reliable witness. Dudley Court Record, NARS.

22. For allegations of military help to Peppin, see testimony of Susan McSween, Washington, Bates, William Bonney, and José Chaves y Chaves. For denials, see testimony of Dudley, Purington, Goodwin, Appel, Keefe,

Lusk, Bush, and Sgt. George Murison. Dudley Court Record, NARS. Several witnesses testified to possemen in military gear; the most convincing was Milo Pierce. Authorized forays: twice Dudley sent details to summon Peppin; twice he sent patrols to notify citizens of his intentions, one through town and another to the foothills; twice he sent soldiers to Ellis's store, once for water from a nearby spring and again to buy chickens for Dudley's supper; and finally, late in the afternoon, he authorized troops to move the furniture out of the Tunstall store.

23. See citations in n. 19. Sam Corbet, the store's clerk, and David Easton tried to get Peppin to stop the looting, but he said he was powerless. It is clear that the store had been ransacked and looting was about to take place. But Milo Pierce, a stockman from the Pecos serving in the posse, intervened. No one, except possibly Jesse Evans, seems to have stolen anything at this time. Both Corbet and Easton admitted this under cross-examination in the Dudley court. Easton further testified that the store was broken into again on the night of July 20, and wagons were parked in front and loaded with merchandise. He described the offenders as mostly Hispanics acting with the resigned acquiescence of Susan McSween, who explained that she would rather have these people have the goods than Peppin's "murderers." With the help of Easton and Corbet, Susan persuaded many of them to return what they had taken, but much of the store's contents disappeared.

24. Chapman to Wallace, Las Vegas, October 24, 1878, Wallace Papers, IHS.

25. Wallace to Hatch, Santa Fe, October 28, 1878, endorsed to Dudley October 30, Exhibit 14, Dudley Court Record, NARS.

26. Dudley to AAAG, DNM, Fort Stanton, November 7 and 9, 1878, enclosing statement of Dr. D. M. Appel, November 9; affidavits of John Long, November 9; Saturnino Baca, November 6; George W. Peppin, November 6; John Priest, November 6; Francisco Gómez, November 6; Lt. G. W. Smith, November 7; and Lt. S. S. Pague, November 7. Dudley to Wallace, Fort Stanton, November 9, 1878. Exhibits 6–13, Dudley Court Record, NARS.

27. Testimony of Wallace, Dudley Court Record, NARS. For Wallace's response to Dudley's affidavits, see Wallace to Hatch, November 14, 1878, and Loud to Dudley, November 15, 1878, Exhibit 63, ibid. For Wallace's proclamation of November 13, 1878, see Records of Territorial Governors: Lew Wallace. TANM, Reel 99, Frames 133–37, NMRCA. The proclamation appeared in the major New Mexico newspapers and also as Exhibit 3, Dudley Court Record, NARS.

28. Dudley to Wallace, Fort Stanton, November 30, 1878, in *New Mexican* (Santa Fe), December 14, 1878. Annexed as Exhibit 2, Dudley Court Record, NARS.

29. Chapman to Wallace, Lincoln, November 25 and 29, 1878, Exhibits 24 and 25, Dudley Court Record, NARS. Wallace to Hatch, Santa Fe, December 7, 1878, with endorsements by Hatch, n.d.; Brig. Gen. John Pope, December 18; Lt. Gen. Philip H. Sheridan, December 21; Gen. William T. Sherman, December 26; and chief clerk of the War Department, January 3, 1879. File 1405 AGO 1878, NARS.

30. Loud to CO Fort Stanton, Santa Fe, October 27, 1878. Wallace to Hatch, Santa Fe, December 14, 1878; Hatch to AAG, DM, Santa Fe, December 17, 1878. File 1405 AGO 1878, NARS. For Chapman's advice to shoot army officers, see Chapman to Wallace, Lincoln, November 25, 1878, Exhibit 25, Dudley Court Record, NARS.

31. Dudley to AAAG, DNM, November 30, December 6, 9, and 17, 1878, File 1405 AGO 1878, NARS.

32. General Order 62, Fort Stanton, December 20, 1878, Exhibit 45, Dudley Court Record, NARS. *Weekly New Mexican* (Santa Fe), January 4, 1879.

33. The proceedings of the military board, including depositions by Chapman and other principals, is Exhibit 28, Dudley Court Record, NARS. See also Dudley to AAAG, DNM, Fort Stanton, December 15 and 17, 1878, Exhibits 79 and 79–13; and Special Order 158, Fort Stanton, December 16, 1878, ibid.

34. Dudley to AAAG, DNM, Fort Stanton, January 26, 1879, RG 393, NARS, LR, DNM, M1088, Reel 36.

35. *Mesilla News*, March 1, 1879. *Las Vegas Gazette*, March 1, 1879. *Las Cruces Thirty-Four*, March 6 and 19, April 9, 1879. *Mesilla Valley Independent*, March 1 and 22, 1879. Dudley to AAAG, DNM, Fort Stanton, February 19, 1879, with enclosures, File 1405 AGO 1878, NARS. The most detailed and authoritative evidence is a newspaper account of the testimony of participants and witnesses in Judge Bristol's court in Mesilla in July 1879. *Mesilla Valley Independent*, July 5, 1879. For a synthesis of the evidence, see Philip J. Rasch, "The Murder of Huston I. Chapman," Los Angeles Westerners, *Brand Book* 8 (1959), pp. 69–82.

36. Dudley to AAAG, DNM, Fort Stanton, February 19, 20, 21, and 24, 1879, with enclosures, File 1405 AGO 1878, NARS. Testimony of Dr. W. B. Lyon, Lee Keyser, B. J. Baca, and Lt. M. F. Goodwin, Dudley Court Record, NARS.

37. Leonard to Wallace, Las Vegas, February 24, 1879, Wallace Papers, IHS.

38. *Mesilla Valley Independent*, July 5, 1879.

39. Before leaving Santa Fe, Hatch informed his superiors that Wallace intended to request Dudley's relief if he found sufficient grounds after reaching Lincoln, and that such a request would probably have to be honored. He

added his own belief that "the present Commanding Officer is unfitted for the Command, complicated as it is with Civil Affairs." Hatch to AAG, DM, Santa Fe, March 2, 1879, RG 393, NARS, LS, DNM, M1072, Reel 6. Hatch was colonel of the regiment of which Dudley was lieutenant colonel, and they had been personal enemies for years. For Dudley's removal, see Wallace to Hatch, Lincoln, March 7, 1879, and Special Field Order No. 2, Hq. DNM in the Field, Fort Stanton, March 8, 1879, Wallace Papers, IHS. For the public meeting of March 8, see testimony of Dr. Spencer H. Gurney and William M. Roberts, Dudley Court Record, NARS.

40. Dudley to Hatch, Fort Stanton, March 9, 1879. Teleg., Dudley to Adjutant General, Fort Stanton, through Mesilla, March 10, 1879. Same to same, through Hq. DM, March 12, 1879. Dudley Court Record, NARS. Dudley to Sherman, Fort Stanton, March 18, 1879, File 1405 AGO 1878, NARS. See also Wallace to Schurz, Lincoln, March 21, 1879, Wallace Papers, IHS.

41. Leonard to Secretary of War, Las Vegas, March 4, 1879, enclosing "charges and specifications" and *Las Vegas Gazette*, March 1, 1879. Special Order 59, Hq. DM, Fort Leavenworth, March 28, 1879. File 1405 AGO 1878. A court of inquiry has no power to convict or sentence; it merely inquires whether sufficient evidence exists to justify a court-martial.

42. Leonard to Wallace, May 20, 1879, Wallace Papers, IHS, recounts the origins of the association between the two.

43. Leonard to Wallace, Fort Stanton, June 6, 1879, tells of getting up a petition for Bristol's removal. Same to same, June 13, touches again on the petition and urges Wallace to take action in the matter now. Wallace to Schurz, Santa Fe, July 23, 1880, puts forward Leonard's name for consideration of the President. All in Wallace Papers, IHS.

44. The Dudley Court Record consists of the daily transcript of the testimony of sixty-four witnesses, extensive exhibits containing mostly official correspondence, the summation of the recorder and the defense counsel, and the findings of the court. For Leonard's impressions, see his letters to Wallace, May 20 and 23, June 6 and 13, 1879, Wallace Papers, IHS.

45. Judge Advocate D. G. Swain to AAG, DM, September 29, 1879; endorsement of Brig. Gen. John Pope, October 15, 1879. Pope to Adjutant General, Fort Leavenworth, October 15, 1879, enclosing charges and specifications; endorsement of Judge Advocate General W. M. Dunn, October 22, 1879; endorsement of chief clerk of the War Department, December 27, 1879; endorsement of Gen. W. T. Sherman, December 30, 1879. Dudley to Adjutant General, Fort Union, October 8, 1879. All in File 1405 AGO 1878, NARS.

46. Lincoln County, District Court, April 1879 term, Criminal Case No. 298, Territory v. John Kinney, N. A. M. Dudley, and George Peppin: arson.

Document file. District Court Journal, pp. 344, 353–56. Doña Ana County, District Court, November 1879 term, Criminal Case No. 533. Document file. District Court Journal, pp. 104, 142, 177–80. Civil Case 176, Susan McSween v. N. A. M. Dudley: libel. Document file. NMSRCA. Dudley to Attorney General Charles Devens, through Hq. of the army, Fort Union, September 16, 1879. Devens to Secretary of War, October 1, 1879. Dudley to Adjutant General, Fort Union, November 4 and December 4, 1879. Teleg., U.S. Attorney Sidney M. Barnes to Attorney General Devens, Mesilla, November 30, 1879. Same to same, Santa Fe, December 4, 1879. File 1405 AGO 1878, NARS. *Mesilla News,* December 6, 1879. *Weekly New Mexican* (Santa Fe), December 6, 1879.

47. See Dudley's personnel file, RG 94, NARS, 6674 ACP 1876. See also *Army and Navy Journal,* May 7, 1910; and *Army and Navy Register,* May 7, 1910.

48. The autobiography is in Dudley's personnel file cited in n. 47.

49. Hatch to Wallace, Santa Fe, April 9, 1879, Wallace Papers, IHS.

4 Lew Wallace

1. There are two standard biographies of Lew Wallace: Irving McKee, *"Ben-Hur" Wallace: The Life of General Lew Wallace* (Berkeley and Los Angeles: University of California Press, 1947); and Robert E. and Katherine M. Morsberger, *Lew Wallace: Militant Romantic* (New York: McGraw Hill, 1980). While both are good, neither is adequate in its treatment of the New Mexico years. For the New Mexico governorship, see Calvin Horn, *New Mexico's Troubled Years: The Story of Early Territorial Governors* (Albuquerque: Horn and Wallace, 1963), pp. 193–97; and Okah L. Jones, "Lew Wallace: Hoosier Governor of Territorial New Mexico, 1878–81," *New Mexico Historical Review* 70 (April 1965), pp. 129–58. There is also some useful material in *Lew Wallace: An Autobiography* (2 vols., New York and London: Harper and Bros., 1906), vol. 2.

2. The letters of English colonizer Montague R. Leverson to President Hayes were important, as were Robert Widenmann's to his father's friend, Secretary of the Interior Carl Schurz. Reverend Taylor F. Ealy wrote to his cousin, Rep. Rush Clark of Pennsylvania, who sent them to the Secretary of War for comment. These and the activities of the British minister are dealt with in Frederick Nolan, ed., *The Life and Death of John Henry Tunstall* (Albuquerque: University of New Mexico Press, 1965). Considerable background is also in Angel's final report: "Report on the Death of John H. Tunstall," in the Department of Justice records in the National Archives,

xerox copy in the Victor Westphall Collection, NMSRCA. The Ealy letters, April 5 and May 3, 1878, are in 1405 AGO 1878, NARS.

3. Schurz to Hayes, August 31, 1878, Hayes Memorial Library, Fremont, Ohio, copy in Fulton Collection, Box 12, Folder 4, UAL. Schurz to Wallace, Washington, D.C., September 4, 1878. Wallace to "Dear Sue" [his wife], Santa Fe, October 8, 1878. Both in Wallace Papers, IHS.

4. Quoted in Morsberger, *Lew Wallace*, p. 264.

5. Teleg., Wallace to Schurz, Santa Fe, October 5, 1878, enclosing Dudley to Hatch, September 29; Bristol to Sherman, October 4; and Sherman to Wallace, October 4. Wallace Papers, IHS.

6. Printed copies, in English and Spanish, are in the Wallace Papers, IHS.

7. Teleg., Wallace to Schurz, Santa Fe, October 14, 1878, Wallace Papers, IHS.

8. Wallace to Hatch, Santa Fe, October 26, 1878. Loud to CO Fort Stanton, Santa Fe, October 27, 1878. Wallace Papers, IHS. Secretary of War George W. McCrary to Gen. W. T. Sherman, Washington, October 8, 1878; disseminated as General Order 74, Hq. of the Army, Adjutant General's Office, same date, File 1405 AGO 1878, NARS.

9. Wallace to Schurz, Santa Fe, October 22, 1878, Wallace Papers, IHS.

10. Wallace's proclamation, November 13, 1878, in both English and Spanish, is in Records of Territorial Governors: Lew Wallace, TANM, Reel 99, Frames 133–37, NMSRCA. See also Wallace to Schurz, Santa Fe, November 13, 1878, Wallace Papers, IHS. Schurz to Wallace, Washington, D.C., December 9, 1878, Wallace Papers, says he knows of no move in the Senate to defeat confirmation. Dudley to AAAG, DNM, Fort Stanton, October 26 and November 2, 1878, Dudley Court Record, NARS, reported an absence of any offenses.

11. *Mesilla Valley Independent*, November 23, 1878. *Mesilla News*, November 23, 1878. *Weekly New Mexican* (Santa Fe), December 7, 1878. Dudley to AAAG, DNM, Fort Stanton, November 16 and 30, December 17, 1878, Dudley Court Record, NARS. Same to same, December 7 and 9, 1878, File 1405 AGO 1878, NARS.

12. Dated November 30, the letter appeared in the *New Mexican* on December 14, 1878.

13. Dudley to Wallace, Fort Stanton, October 10, 1878; Chapman to Wallace, Las Vegas, October 24, 1878, Lew Wallace Papers. Wallace to Hatch, Santa Fe, October 28, 1878; Dudley to AAAG, DNM, Fort Stanton, November 7 and 9, 1878, with enclosures; Wallace to Dudley, Santa Fe, November 16 and 30, 1878; Chapman to Wallace, Lincoln, November 25 and 29, 1878, Dudley Court Record, NARS. Wallace to Hatch, December 7, 1878, File 1405 AGO 1878, NARS.

14. This is speculation, of course, but throughout Wallace's tenure Sherman displayed a notable coolness toward his old comrade-in-arms. At each level above Hatch—General John Pope at Fort Leavenworth and General Philip Sheridan in Chicago—Wallace's proposal was condemned but referred to higher levels for action. See endorsements on Wallace to Hatch, December 7, 1878, File 1405 AGO 1878, NARS.

15. Wallace to Schurz, Santa Fe, October 1 and December 21, 1878, Wallace Papers, IHS. Chapman to Wallace, Lincoln, November 25 and 29, 1878, Dudley Court Record, NARS. *Mesilla News*, November 23, 1878. *Mesilla Valley Independent*, same date. Dudley's open letter scored Wallace for being in the territory for eight weeks without getting closer than two hundred miles to the "scene of the terrible death struggles."

16. Wallace, *Autobiography*, vol. 2, pp. 935–36, paints a graphic picture of the setting in which he wrote the eighth and last book of *Ben-Hur*.

17. Dudley to AAAG, DNM, Fort Stanton, November 30, December 8 and 24, 1878, Exhibits 23, 79–6, and 79–17, Dudley Court Record, NARS. Same to same, December 7, 1878, File 1405 AGO 1878, NARS. Same to same, January 26, 1879, RG 393, NARS, LR, Hq. DNM, M1088, Reel 36.

18. Hatch to AAG, DM, Santa Fe, December 17, 1878; Wallace to Hatch, Santa Fe, February 14, 1879; Hatch to AAG, DM, February 17, 1879; endorsement of Brig. Gen. John Pope, February 24, 1879; endorsement of Gen. W. T. Sherman, March 6; endorsement of chief clerk of War Department, March 12, File 1405 AGO 1878, NARS. Wallace advised Wilson that U.S. Marshal John Sherman refused to appoint a deputy marshal in Lincoln. Wallace to Wilson, Santa Fe, February 6, 1879, Wallace Papers, IHS.

19. *Weekly New Mexican* (Santa Fe), February 8, 1879.

20. J. H. Watts to Wallace, Fort Stanton, February 24, 1879, Wallace Papers, IHS.

21. Wallace to John B. Wilson, Santa Fe, January 18, 1878, Wallace Papers, IHS.

22. *Mesilla News*, March 1, 1879. *Las Vegas Gazette*, March 1, 1879. *Las Cruces Thirty-Four*, March 6 and 19, April 9, 1879. *Mesilla Valley Independent*, March 1 and 22, 1879. Dudley to AAAG, DNM, Fort Stanton, February 19, 1879, with enclosures, File 1405 AGO 1878, IHS. The most detailed and authoritative evidence is a newspaper account of the testimony of participants and witnesses in Judge Bristol's court in Mesilla in July 1879. *Mesilla Valley Independent*, July 5, 1879. For a synthesis of the evidence, see Philip J. Rasch, "The Murder of Huston I. Chapman," Los Angeles Westerners, *Brand Book* 8 (1959), pp. 69–82.

23. Dudley Court Record, NARS: Kimball to Dudley, Lincoln, February 19, 1879, Exhibit 79–40; Special Order 26, Fort Stanton, February 19,

Exhibit 79–39; Petition of citizens to Dudley, Lincoln, February 19, Exhibit 59; Dudley to AAAG, DNM, Fort Stanton, February 20 and 21, Exhibits 79–44 and 79–43; Goodwin to Post Adjutant, Fort Stanton, February 23, Exhibit 54.

24. Wallace to Schurz, Santa Fe, February 27, 1879, Wallace Papers, IHS. Wallace to Hatch, Santa Fe, February 27, 1879, File 1405 AGO 1878, NARS. Hatch to AAG, DM, Santa Fe, March 2, 1879, RG 393, NARS, LS, Hq. DNM, M1072, Reel 6.

25. Hatch to AAG, DM, Santa Fe, March 2, 1879, RG 393, NARS, LS, Hq. DNM, M1072, Reel 6.

26. Wallace to Hatch, Lincoln, March 7, 1879. Special Field Order No. 2, Hq. DNM, March 8, 1879. Wallace to Hatch, Lincoln, March 9, 1879. Wallace Papers, IHS. For Carroll, see his personnel file in RG 94, NARS, 3754 ACP 1874. For the public meeting of March 8, see testimony of Dr. Spencer H. Gurney and William M. Roberts, Dudley Court Record, NARS.

27. Wallace to Carroll, Lincoln, March 11 and 12, 1879. Wallace Papers, IHS. A number of fragmentary notes in this collection record names and other information obtained from these sources. Justice Wilson was a prominent informant.

28. Wallace to Hatch, Lincoln, March 5, 1879. Wallace to Carroll, Lincoln, March 10, 1879. Carroll to Wallace, March 11, 1879. Dolan to Wallace, Fort Stanton, March 14, 1879. Wallace to Schurz, Lincoln, March 21, 1879. Wallace Papers, IHS. Carroll to AAAG, DNM, Fort Stanton, March 15, 1879, RG 393, NARS, LR, Hq. DNM, M1088, Reel 36. Hatch to Goodwin, Fort Stanton, March 6, 1879, Exhibit 79–57, Dudley Court Record, NARS. Anonymous letter from Fort Stanton, March 13, 1879, in *Las Cruces Thirty-Four,* March 19, 1879.

29. Wallace to Schurz, March 31, 1879, Wallace Papers, IHS. "Rio Bonito" to Ed., Fort Stanton, April 8, 1879, *Mesilla Valley Independent,* April 12, 1879.

30. Wallace to Hatch, Lincoln, March 6, 1879, Wallace Papers, IHS.

31. Wallace to J. B. Wilson, Fort Stanton, March 8, 1879, Wallace Papers, IHS.

32. The exchange of correspondence, together with a lengthy and informative set of notes that Wallace made of Bonney's knowledge of people and events, are in the Wallace Papers. See also Philip J. Rasch, "The Governor Meets the Kid," English Westerners, *Brand Book* 8 (April 1966), pp. 5–12. For the escape of Campbell and Evans, see *Mesilla Independent,* April 5, 1879.

33. Wallace to Schurz, Lincoln, March 21 and 31, 1879. Bristol to Wallace, Mesilla, March 16, 1879. Wallace Papers, IHS. *Mesilla Valley Independent,* March 22, 1879.

34. Wallace to Hatch, Lincoln, March 9, 1879. Wallace to Purington, Lincoln, March 21, 1879 (three messages). Purington to Wallace, Fort Stanton, same date (three replies). Wallace to Schurz, Lincoln, March 31, 1879. Hatch to Purington, El Paso, March 18, 1879. Loud to Purington, Santa Fe, March 19, 1879. RG 393, NARS, LS, Hq. DNM, M1072, Reel 6.

35. Campaign Records, Lincoln County Rifles, 1879, TANM, Reel 87, Frames 185–202. Patrón to Wallace, Santa Fe, January 10, 1880 (Patrón's final report), Records of the Territorial Governors: Lew Wallace, ibid., Reel 99, Frames 20–21. Both in NMSRCA. The Wallace Papers contain numerous exchanges between Patrón and Wallace during the governor's stay in Lincoln. See also J. B. Wilson to Wallace, May 18, 1879, Wallace Papers, IHS, and *Weekly New Mexican* (Santa Fe), May 17, 1879.

36. Wallace to Schurz, Lincoln, March 31, 1879. Wallace to Hayes, through Schurz, same date. Wallace Papers, IHS.

37. Wallace to Schurz, Lincoln, April 4, 1879. Wallace to Bristol, same date. Wallace Papers, IHS.

38. Wallace to Schurz, Lincoln, March 31, 1879. Wallace to Waldo, Lincoln, April 3, 1879. Leonard to Wallace, Lincoln, May 20, 1879, recounts the origins of their association. Wallace Papers, IHS.

39. Wallace to Schurz, Lincoln, April 18, 1879, Wallace Papers, IHS.

40. Lincoln County, District Court, April 1879 term, District Court Journal, 1875–79, pp. 296–387, NMSRCA. Wallace to Leonard, Fort Stanton, April 13, 1879. J. B. Wilson to Wallace, Lincoln, April 21, 1879. Leonard to Wallace, Lincoln, April 20 and May 20, 1879. Wallace Papers, IHS.

41. *Mesilla Valley Independent*, May 10, 1879. *Weekly New Mexican* (Santa Fe), May 17, 1879. Purington to AAAG, DNM, Fort Stanton, May 3, 1879. Leonard to Wallace, Lincoln, May 20, 1879. Wallace Papers, IHS.

42. See Wallace's testimony and Waldo's summation, Dudley Court Record, NARS.

43. Wallace to Schurz, Santa Fe, June 11, 1879, Wallace Papers, IHS.

44. Hatch's superior, Brig. Gen. John Pope, wanted Maj. James F. Wade relieved from recruiting duty and sent to New Mexico. Wade belonged to Hatch's regiment, the Ninth Cavalry, and the substitution could have been easily arranged. Pope endorsement, March 8, 1879, on Wallace to Hatch, February 27, 1879, File 1405 AGO 1878, NARS.

45. Wallace to Susan Wallace, Santa Fe, December 4, 1879, Wallace Papers, IHS.

Note
on Sources

In large part because of the involvement of Billy the Kid, the Lincoln County War has inspired a huge literature. The standard works, cited by nearly all authorities, are William A. Keleher, *Violence in Lincoln County, 1869–1881: A New Mexico Item* (Albuquerque: University of New Mexico Press, 1957; 2d ed., with introduction by C. L. Sonnichsen, 1982), and Robert N. Mullin, ed., *Maurice Garland Fulton's History of the Lincoln County War* (Tucson: University of Arizona Press, 1968). While of great value, both are deficient in organization, synthesis, and documentation. More reliable is a series of articles by Philip J. Rasch, appearing mostly in publications of various corrals of the Westerners, some of which are cited in the footnotes. Possessing hardly more than a shadow of redeeming value is Walter Noble Burns's enormously successful *Saga of Billy the Kid* (New York: Doubleday, Page & Co., 1926).

In general, the published reminiscences of participants are full of misinformation and useful chiefly for local color and personality portraits. Among these are George W. Coe, *Frontier Fighter, the Autobiography of George W. Coe,* as related to Nan Hillary Harrison (Boston and New York: Houghton Mifflin Company, 1934; 2d ed., Albuquerque: University of New Mexico Press, 1951; Lakeside Classics ed., ed. by Doyce B. Nunis, Jr., Chicago: L. L. Donnelly and Co., 1984); Pat F. Garrett, *Authentic Life of Billy the Kid* (Santa Fe: New Mexican Printing Co., 1882; ed. Maurice Garland Fulton, New York: Macmillan, 1927; ed. Jeff C. Dykes, Norman: University of Oklahoma Press, 1954); Miguel A. Otero, *My Life on the Frontier, 1864–1882* (New York: Press of the Pioneers, 1935); Miguel A. Otero, *The Real Billy the Kid: With New Light on the Lincoln County War* (New York: Rufus Rockwell Wilson, 1936); and George W. Curry, *An Autobiography* (Albuquerque: University of New Mexico Press, 1958). Lily Klasner, *My Girlhood among Outlaws,* ed. Eve Ball (Tucson: University of Arizona Press, 1972) is especially good for characterizations.

A cross between narrative and documentary history is Frederick W. Nolan, ed., *The Life and Death of John Henry Tunstall* (Albuquerque: University of New Mexico Press, 1965). It contains long excerpts from Tunstall's letters to his family in London, with commentary by Nolan. The origins of the Lincoln County War cannot be understood without constant resort to this work.

Perhaps the least appreciated and most valuable body of source material lies in the records of the U.S. Army. After Colonel Dudley took command of Fort Stanton, he was ordered to submit weekly reports on civil disorders in Lincoln County. This he did conscientiously, pouring forth long descriptions of people and events and appending a variety of documents from civilian sources that came to him. These and other documents relating to the Lincoln County War found their way into a special file in the Adjutant General's Office in Washington, D.C. Its designation is RG 94, NARS, AGO, LR (Main Series), 1871–80, File 1405 AGO 1878, available on microfilm as M666, Reels 397 and 398. Other important military records include: RG 393, LR, Hq. DNM, on microfilm as M1088; and the same, LS, M1072; RG 153, NARS, Judge Advocate General's Office, Records Relating to the Dudley Inquiry (CQ 1284); and the records of the post of Fort Stanton, RG 393, NARS (not on microfilm). The monthly Fort Stanton post returns, recording troop and other statistics as well as events of the month, are available on microfilm.

Less bountiful are the Interior Department records. The territorial governor reported to the Secretary of the Interior. Pertinent are RG 75, NARS, Office of Indian Affairs, LR, on microfilm as M234; RG 75, NARS, Office of Indian Affairs, Records of the New Mexico Superintendency, 1849–80, on microfilm as T21; RG 48, NARS, Interior Department Territorial Records: New Mexico, M364; and RG 48, Interior Department Appointment Papers, M750. For Governor Lew Wallace, his personal papers at the Indiana Historical Society in Indianapolis are unusually rich in documenting his role in the concluding stages of the war. His reports to the Secretary of the Interior are in his papers as well as in the official records.

The voluminous report of Frank Warner Angel, special agent of the Departments of Justice and the Interior, is essential to reconstructing the origins and early progress of the Lincoln County War. Although Angel had prejudices that have to be kept in mind, his report is full of depositions by prominent figures in the war, which were sworn within weeks of the events testified to. Submitted in October 1878, it is entitled "Report on the Death of John H. Tunstall," and is in the Records of the Department of Justice, NARS. A complete copy is in the Westphall Collection, NMSRCA.

The NMSRCA contains indispensable records. Most valuable are those of the Third Judicial District Court in Mesilla, which sat in Lincoln County twice a year and tried the cases growing out of the Lincoln County War. This depository also houses the Territorial Archives of New Mexico, including records of the territorial governors. The territorial district court also functioned as federal district court; records of federal cases are in the DFRC. This depository also has records of the Mescalero Apache Indian Agency, which are sometimes helpful.

The territorial newspapers, for all their rhetorical excess, are necessary sources. They published letters from the scene, usually by anonymous correspondents, and when shorn of bias they help in establishing the chronology and course of major events. The most helpful are the *Mesilla Valley Independent* and the *Mesilla News,* although the latter's rabid partisanship has to be discounted. Albert J. Fountain edited the *Independent* and, as a lawyer and sometime officer of the district court, brought first-hand knowledge to his dispatches. Also of value are Cimarron *News and Press, Las Vegas Gazette,* Santa Fe *New Mexican,* Silver City *Grant County Herald,* and Las Cruces *Thirty-Four.*

Finally, any serious researchers in this field must acknowledge a large debt to the lifelong acquisitive habits of Maurice Garland Fulton and Robert N. Mullin. Fulton, an English professor at New Mexico Military Institute in Roswell, devoted decades to collecting and studying Lincoln County material, and he interviewed and corresponded with many of the participants. Mullin, an oil executive, also amassed mountains of documents. Fulton's collection is now at the University Arizona Library, which also houses papers of the Blazer family, owners of Blazer's Mills, and Rev. Taylor F. Ealy and his wife. Ealy came to Lincoln at McSween's invitation and observed the first few months of the war. Many of his papers are set forth in Norman J. Bender, ed., *Missionaries, Outlaws, and Indians: Taylor F. Ealy at Lincoln and Zuñi, 1878–1881* (Albuqerque: University of New Mexico Press, 1984). Mullin's collection is housed in the J. Evetts Haley History Center, Midland, Texas. Haley himself interviewed participants in the Lincoln County War in the 1920s. The transcripts are in the Haley Center.

For the historian, the Lincoln County War offers a formidable challenge. Virtually all of the primary material, both contemporary and reminiscent, is tainted with partisanship. Much of the secondary literature reflects this partisanship and is also more or less encumbered by the mythology of Billy the Kid. Yet for the diligent researcher the story is there, waiting to be extracted, piece by piece, from the overburden of passion and prejudice. Few historical episodes of similar scope have bequeathed to posterity such a rich trove of the ores from which history is refined.

Index

Copeland, John, 14, 28–30, 43
Corbet, Sam, 27
courts: favoritism of, 7, 23; grand
 juries, 13, 28, 36, 57, 74;
 paralysis of, 64, 67, 71–74;
 retrials and change of venue, 37,
 57
cow camp incident, 16, 29

Dolan, James J., 3, 6, 9, 11, 13,
 22, 35, 43, 54, 70, 74; attack on
 McSween, 7–8; posse of, 14–17
Dudley, Nathan A. M., 15, 32, 47,
 51–53, 63–65; arrival in Lincoln,
 42; the balance of war and, 44,
 48–50; death of, 58; motives of,
 33, 34, 48, 50; removal of, 36,
 55–58, 66, 69

Ealy, Taylor F., 16, 27
Ellis, Isaac, 46
embezzlement charge, 7, 13, 23, 28
Evans, Jesse, 6, 9, 10, 24, 32, 35,
 36, 48, 70, 71; Billy the Kid
 and, 22

Fairview, 70
federal (military) actions, 29, 32,
 64, 67, 75; canon at Lincoln,
 45, 46, 47, 49; after Chapman
 killing, 54; Congressional
 withdrawal of, 17, 31; inquiry
 from Washington, 16; reviewed,
 43; soldier posses, 10–18, 30. *See
 also* Dudley, Nathan A. M.
Five-Day Battle, 18, 32, 41
Fort Grant, 22
Fort Stanton, 3, 13, 25, 44. *See
 also* Dudley, Nathan A. M. *and*
 federal (military) actions
French, James H. (Jim), 26, 27,
 32, 54

Fritz, Charles, 8, 34
Fritz, Emil, 7

Garfield, James A., 77
Garrett, Pat, 37
Gauss, Godfrey, 23
Godfroy, Frederick C., 33, 34
government contracts, 3, 4
governor's militia, 72
grand juries, 13, 28, 36, 57, 74.
 See also courts
Grant, Ulysses S., 62

Hatch, Edward, 16, 36, 52, 53, 55,
 58, 63, 64, 66, 69
Hayes, Rutherford B., 11, 16, 43,
 52, 56, 61, 62, 64, 76
Hill, Tom, 24
Hindman, George, 26
Hispanics, 2, 12, 27, 32, 44, 72;
 with Peppin, 31; with the
 Regulators, 25, 29–33
House, The, 2–9

Independence Day skirmish, 17, 31
Indian Agency stock theft, 33

J. H. Tunstall & Co., 5
Jas. J. Dolan & Co., 6
Johnson, William H., 28

Kid Antrim, 9, 22. *See also* Billy
 the Kid
Kimball, George, 36, 54
Kinney, John, 17, 30
Kruling, "Dutch Charlie," 28

L. G. Murphy & Co., 6
Leonard, Ira E., 55–57, 73, 74
Leverson, Montague R., 16
Lincoln, the county seat, 2
Lincoln County Bank, 5